NO HYPERBOLE

The New Rules Of Online Business

No Hyperbole: The New Rules of Online Business by Sean Kaye

ISBN: 978-0-9945824-1-6

© 2018 Sean Kaye

Published by Casual Marketer

35B Abbott Street, Cammeray, NSW, Australia 2062

casualmarketer.com

This book and the content provided herein are simply for educational and entertainment purposes, and do not take the place of legal or financial advice from your lawyer or accountant.

Every effort has been made to ensure that the content provided in this book is accurate and helpful for the reader at the time of publishing. However, this is book is not an exhaustive treatment of the subjects. No liability is assumed for losses or damages due to the information provided. You are responsible for your own choices, actions, and results.

For permissions contact:

support@rapidactionsupport.com

Table of Contents

PREAMBLE   5

INTRODUCTION   9

SECTION 1   21

THE "BE" AND "DO" RULES   21

  Be a Good Person   22

  Be a Student of the Game   25

  Become An Authority, Experts Are Overrated   29

  Do One Thing At A Time (and Do It Well)   34

Section 2   40

THE "DON'T" RULES   40

  Don't Be A Digital Sharecropper   41

  Don't Be The Conductor Of The Free Train!   47

  Don't Be Homer   51

  Don't Get Caught Buying Hope   56

Section 3   62

The Intimate Relationship Between Sales and Delivery   62

  Nothing Happens Until Someone Sells Something   63

  Thou Shalt Know Thy Market   68

  Attract Ideal Customers, Repel Everybody Else   73

  Referrals: The Second Most Powerful Force In The Universe   78

  Under Promise and Over Deliver   82

  People Will Buy Good Experience   87

Section 4   93

Rules for Business Builders   93

The Marketing Law Of Levers   94

Educate and Indoctrinate Your Audience   97

Make It Easy For People To Give You Their Money   103

You're In The Traffic Business   107

Plant Corn, Not Baseball Fields   113

Pricing Is Hard And You Will Get It Wrong   117

Beware Vanity Metrics   122

Pay Peanuts, Get Monkeys   128

Section 5   **133**

Rules You Should Know and Never Forget   **133**

Put Down Your Technology Toys   134

Consume What You Buy, Don't Be A Collector   139

Minimum Viable Product Is Not Code For Garbage   143

Master The Pareto Principle   148

Perfect Is The Enemy Of Good Enough   152

Model Success, Don't Rip It Off   157

Fire Crappy Customers   161

Accountability Partners Are For Losers   167

AdSense Is Arbitrage For Stupid People   172

It's Your House, Everyone Else Is A Guest   176

CONCLUSION   179

BONUSES AND EXTRAS   182

PREAMBLE

This is the second time I've written this preamble – the first time was on January 1st, 2017 which was about a year after I originally completed the book. This time it's March 9th, 2018 and I'm determined to get this book out the door and published to a wider audience.

It's been quite a ride.

When I wrote this book, it was meant to be as a free gift to people who joined the, as then not yet created, Casual Marketer Monthly Newsletter. I had intended to just pull these rules together, get them quickly printed off and send them out to people as they joined.

But then my friend Scott Duffy suggested that I turn this into a "proper book". That started a long-winded process until finally I managed to print off a small run of special edition copies for my newsletter members back in mid-2016.

So much has changed since then that I really need this preamble to fill in the backstory.

The Casual Marketer Monthly Newsletter was a physical product that ran for a full two years with 24 editions being published. By November 2017, I just wasn't "feeling it" anymore and decided to cease publication and so one morning I woke up and cancelled the over 100+ recurring subscriptions.

My ambition for Casual Marketer has always been as some sort of modern publishing company where I share my experience and business insights in a variety of modalities with people who are building online businesses either full-time or as a side hustle project.

To that end, in December 2017, having shut down the physical newsletter, I decided to pivot towards creating more information products and writing books which is more aligned with my interests personally and as a publisher.

At the time of writing this version of the preamble I have written over one million words for Casual Marketer via my daily emails, this book, and the newsletters. I also have over 100,000 customers who have taken my various video training products (including nearly 80,000 students on Udemy alone).

It's been an interesting journey to this point and I'm very excited to be FINALLY getting this book into your hands. I'd also like to add that I'm extraordinarily grateful that you've chosen to read it and I hope it helps you on your journey.

As a token of my appreciation, I've created a "special chapter" that's not in the book that you can download if you go to: https://nohyperbole.com/specialchapter

I wrote the bonus chapter in early 2017 in reaction to the craziness that social media had become. The takeaway action is handy for you to learn how to use the social media zeitgeist to your advantage – I highly recommend you take the time to download and read it.

In closing, I'd like to thank my lovely wife Harriet and my son Zac who put up with me spending a lot of time at the computer and staring at my phone. My mom, Jean, who gave me more than I could ever repay. My mother-in-law, Genevieve, for being so supportive and reminding me all the time to "write these things down."

I'm also blessed with having some very smart friends and supporters who inspire, help and encourage me: Scott Duffy,

James Schramko, Barry Moore, Jake Hower, Ben Settle, John Romaine, Nicole English, Alycia Edgar, and a bunch of other folks who are too numerous to name, but thank you all the same.

INTRODUCTION

Let me take you back to the year 2006.

I was tasked with setting up and running not one but two new
technology businesses by my boss. One of those companies was
a Software-as-a-Service business that we were acquiring
because it did document control and project management for
about $10B worth of construction and mining projects which
were our core business. The other was a brand new idea to
build a "managed services" company to host the SaaS
application as well as provide other services for our corporate
subsidiary businesses and external 3rd party companies.

These businesses were given a couple of mandates: one, be
better than anything we could buy on the market thus reducing
the company's risk; and two, they needed to be able to stand on
their own two feet and be cash flow profitable.

Then I was effectively given $10m of "startup capital" to get on
with it.

The managed services business would be almost what you'd call a "private cloud provider" in today's modern technology vocabulary. We were easily five years ahead of the market. We were selling consumption based compute and storage on demand and within two years we'd gone from an idea to doing $40m of revenue annually. Along the way, we bought a technology security business for $6m and started providing services to big banks.

The software-as-a-service business was really interesting. For the first two years that I oversaw this business revenue growth was largely stagnant and we weren't seeing the improvement in application performance we wanted. We were pulling $1m/yr in revenue and licensing the core technology we were using. It was a mess to be candid with you, we'd stabilized the situation and removed risk just by fixing the underlying platform, but the application we were licensing wasn't going to cut it.

So I went back to my boss and got another $3m to re-write the SaaS app and fix it.

He gave us the money and one year to re-write this massive software product from a standing start. This was a tool that was by this stage managing documents and project communications for $15B of construction work across Australia and into Asia and the Middle East. He also wanted us to grow that business fivefold in 18 months.

This is where the story gets interesting.

We had about 10,000 monthly paid users and our sales methodology was non-existent. Our largest competitor in the SaaS space had just finished raising $65m in venture capital from the US and they were growing everywhere. If that wasn't enough of a challenge, our publicly listed parent company was also a competitor to almost all of our potential customers which added substantial levels of sales complexity.

The only way to grow and meet our targets was to find a new way of doing things.

This is where I discovered online marketing.

We looked at companies like Basecamp that were making a name for themselves and other startups from that era, but we just didn't see that type of approach working for us.

We were getting ready to launch our new product and I started searching for ideas on how to do a product launch. I stumbled onto Jeff Walker's "Product Launch Formula."

I immediately bought it and devoured it. I ended up on Jeff's list (which I am still on today) and then came across people like Frank Kern, Jeff Johnson, Andy Jenkins and John Reese.

Irrespective of what you think of these people today in 2015 as I write this, back then, they were pioneers. They were bringing traditional direct marketing approaches to the internet.

Product positioning, understanding your market, writing compelling copy and having good hooks were the foundation of what they were doing. I understood those things and what they were able to show me is how to move that to the internet. Building email lists, using video, understanding search engine optimization and the power of affiliate marketing were concepts they were fusing into those traditional approaches.

I bought and consumed their products (the consumed part is stupidly importantly), went to their events overseas, met tons of interesting people and worked out how to apply what they were doing to help grow the businesses I was running.

The product we were building launched successfully. Like all software it had teething problems, but that's life. We created blog posts, we gamed the search engines, we bought ads from Google and we did a series of live events across Australia, Hong Kong and Dubai.

We went from 10,000 monthly paid users to over 35,000, our email list grew from 15,000 to 75,000 and the value of the construction and engineering projects our software was being used on went from $10B to over $50B. Most importantly, by the time I left in late 2010, we'd gone from $1m in revenue to about $11m while being very profitable.

This wasn't all down to the online marketing techniques I'd learned, I also had amazing people. My staff were smart, motivated and hardworking. The developers we hired here in Sydney were putting in 12 hour days often six days a week to meet the deadline for the product.

And that's a point I have to stress, it doesn't matter what you know or how smart you are, your success is largely predicated on the people around you and that includes your family. If you're a casual marketer, you might be on this online business journey on your own, but your family are coming with you no matter what, never forget that!

When I finally finished up that four-year episode of running those two businesses, I was utterly exhausted and really struggling physically. TripAdvisor tells me that during that time I'd visited 79 cities in 25 countries and travelled over 530,000km - for some perspective, that's a round trip to the moon and half way there again. That takes a toll.

I'd had food poisoning in Chile, came down with Swine Flu in Paris and one time I woke up in Berlin at the Hilton Hotel in Potsdamerplatz and called the reception to ask which city I was in. At the same time, I've been to places and seen things that most people only dream about, all for free, staying in five star hotels and flying first or business class, so it wasn't all bad.

In 2009, I started dabbling with my own online business ideas based on what I'd learned, but I was so busy and tired that it was nothing more than tinkering. In late 2010, I made the decision to get more serious about it and in early 2011 when I left my employer, I spent 18 months working on my own online business.

Successes, failures and everything in between happened during that time. It was interesting and it really recharged my batteries.

But I got bored.

I decided in late 2012 to go back to work.

For most people, they wouldn't understand this at all. I was free of the day-to-day grind of having a job, why on earth would I go back to it?

Well, I liked doing business online, but I liked what I did professionally more. I play with big technology and really cutting edge stuff. I solve technology problems on a global scale worth millions of dollars.

I just liked it.

Are there things that I dislike about working full-time? Sure. You can pick holes in everything, but having had the time and opportunity to compare the two lifestyles, I decided I liked working.

I also decided to do both and that's where the idea for Casual Marketer ultimately comes from. The desire to work full-time but also have a nice little business on the side appeals to me, so I structure my online business activities to suit that.

With that said, I know that's not for everyone. I would say that the vast majority of people reading this probably would like to replace their work income with something online and get the hell out of the rat race.

And this is where I'm going to try and help you.

Over my years of doing online marketing in various niches and business models, I've gained a vast array of experience and knowledge. I have also run real businesses and I've had successes and failures in both.

What I'm trying to do with this book is to share some simple rules that you need to know and follow to improve your overall chance of success. Many of these rules fly in the face of conventional "internet marketing" wisdom, but to be honest, that's a good thing because most of that wisdom is wrong or is its own form of marketing to try and sell you something.

I call this book "No Hyperbole: The New Rules For Online Business" and it's squarely aimed at fast tracking your knowledge and helping you to avoid the pitfalls that you can drop into that derail most people. These rules are maxims and idioms that I've come up with or heard over the years that I've written down or mentally filed away to help myself keep on the right path. I've also realized from talking to many, many people over the years who are just starting out that these ideas can help people in that situation as well.

You should "consume" this material, in fact that's one of the rules. There's no point in you getting this information and sticking it on a shelf somewhere. I can absolutely guarantee that you will not learn these lessons by osmosis. You're going to have to read them and probably re-read them a couple more times, maybe even highlight a few things, flag some pages for future reference and basically study this stuff to really get it. Do it enough and it will become muscle memory.

And with that, let's get on with the rules.

STRUCTURE OF THE BOOK

The original draft of this book was just a shopping list of rules. After I completed the first draft I realized that I probably needed to put more structure around it and some of the rules naturally gravitated towards each other. For the second draft, I rejigged everything into the format you see now.

I've grouped the rules into Sections around a specific theme. The rules themselves all work in a standalone fashion, but as I mentioned there are some that work well in concert.

Are these groupings perfect? No. Do some of the rules straddle multiple Sections? Yes.

If these things bother you, then before we begin I suggest you flip right away to the rules "Perfect is the Enemy of Good Enough" and "It's Your House, Everyone Else is a Guest" as these will deliver you the most value right away.

Now that we've cleared up that these groupings aren't perfect and I'm the one writing the book so I get to decide how it's structured, it's time to get on with the show.

Section 1: The "BE" and "DO" Rules

This section is pretty straightforward; these are rules around your behavior. They are positive ways of looking at how you act and what you do. These rules are intentionally at the front of the book because they are foundational in nature - you will be more successful, if you follow these rules as the basis of what you do in business.

Section 2: The "DON'T" Rules

It would be overly simplistic to say that this group of rules are the antithesis of the rules in the first section. These are really lessons I've learned over the years about mistakes that I've made and seen others make. Remembering these rules will help you avoid hitting the same potholes.

Section 3: The Intimate Relationship Between Sales and Delivery

Someone recently told me in a discussion around a sales opportunity that I was "confusing sales with delivery". The implication was that sell first and then worry about delivery. I get that perspective; I just think it's fundamentally wrong. I believe being focused on delivery at the highest level empowers your selling, it doesn't confuse it. These rules outline this relationship.

Section 4: Rules for Business Builders

These rules are pretty simple; they are designed to help you maintain focus on building a strong business with solid strategic foundations. This section is all about building, measuring and managing assets that will drive the real value in your business.

Section 5: Rules You Should Know and Never Forget

I admit it, these rules are a bit of a catch-all. There are some very good lessons and ideas, but these rules are really the maxims portion of the book. This section is somewhat more philosophical about how you do things with a slightly larger focus on mindset

SECTION 1
THE "BE" AND "DO" RULES

Be a Good Person

Let's start this book with what I consider to be the most important rule not just in business, but in life in general. You should always strive to be the best person that you can be. Things like honesty, fairness and being respectful to people cost you nothing, but pay dividends that go well beyond the confines of revenue and profit.

To be completely blunt, this is the primary rule I've always had in business. I only work with good people. I'm not talking about the most talented writers or the best software developers; I mean genuinely good human beings.

It probably seems like one of those rules where you're sitting there going, "Duh... Of course we should only do business with good people", but the reality is that in the online world, there seems to be a higher proportion of frauds, charlatans and outright scoundrels than in your day-to-day in-person business experiences. The anonymity and physical separation makes it easier I think for people to try to lie, cheat and steal. As a result, you need to keep your guard up a bit more.

And this works both ways, you need to be a good person when you deal with others as well. You need to remember that the person looking at your site or sending you an email is a real human being. This person has their own goals, aspirations and desires. They have a family and friends. Again, it may seem really simplistic, but it is imperative that you never lose sight of this rule.

I find over time it has become easier to spot the really good people, the ones with integrity who are able to give trust as well as maintain it. For me, there are a couple of things I think about when I meet a new entrepreneur I'm thinking of working with:

How did I come in contact with this person? Were they referred to me by someone I trust already? Are they a cold lead? What's the context? Is this person someone I want to do business with or have they approached me? What is their driving ambition for establishing this relationship? Do our desired outcomes align with respect to this engagement?

It might seem a bit over-the-top especially when you consider that I view customers through this prism as well, but the reality is, establishing a working relationship with someone who isn't a good person is both personally taxing and financially draining.

Having to deal with customers that aren't nice human beings is tough for everyone and it never ends well.

When I'm initiating the relationship, I always try and establish my motives and bona fides upfront. I explain what I'm looking to get from working with this person, how I see this impacting us collectively and individually and what value we can derive for our customers and stakeholders by having this relationship. I'm really big on value creation, I think it is important that if I start working with someone there should be wins for everyone, not just our bank balances.

Ultimately, what you're looking for are people who share your sense of ethics and who place a value on working with good people and being a good human being themselves. I don't know about you, but that really doesn't seem like too high of hurdle to set for people you do business with.

Takeaway Item: Being a good person will always make you more money in the long run. Look to do business with people that share your sense of fairness and who look to create things that are of value for other people as well as themselves.

Be a Student of the Game

One thing that you often hear online marketing gurus say is, "You don't need to be on anyone else's list besides mine." That always makes me laugh because it has nothing to do with you, it has to do with them. They don't want you wandering off and looking at something else that may be sexier than what they're offering. It's about their share of your wallet and nothing else.

On the other hand, I encourage everyone reading this to join other people's lists, go watch their videos, read blogs and buy products you think might help you get to the next step in your journey.

Why do I suggest that?

First of all, I've got an abundance based mindset around everything. I don't need to "own" my customers, I need to serve them and help them by sharing what I know. Telling you to ignore everything else that is going on is selfish and predicated on a scarcity mindset. It says that you only have so much money to spend, so I want all of it. That's dumb.

Secondly, it stinks of a lack of confidence. On the surface it might appear that this person is saying, "Hey, I can teach you everything you need to know, I'm just that awesome" but the reality is, they're fearful you'll find someone else who resonates with you more. They're afraid of being shown as inferior.

And lastly, I believe that to become the best at your craft, you need to become a student of the game and lift your domain IQ. There is no way that any single person can teach you everything you need to know to be successful, you need to be out there learning from lots of sources.

This leads into my philosophy of learning in general.

It is vitally important that you learn from people that are doing what you want to do very well, but you also need to watch people who are doing it poorly. I learn so much from watching people do things badly, it's actually one of the ways I learn best. Being exposed to people who do something poorly or are making mistakes makes it that much easier to identify when people are doing things really well.

And the only way to get that perspective is to experience it all first hand. You need to be watching and learning all the time.

This is why athletes watch so much footage - their coaches show them where they do things wrong and then show them the right way.

This is a form of situational awareness. If you can identify a situation and you've seen both the right way and the wrong way to do something, you're more likely to do it right. That's not just relevant to basketball or rugby, that completely applies to your online business as well.

Now, let me toss out a couple things you need to remember.

One problem that I see all the time with people is that they become full-time students of other people's online businesses. I can honestly say that I've lost count of the number of people I've run across who tell me they've been studying for two or three years without having taken any kind of action. Don't be that person.

There are also people who study so many things concurrently that they totally overwhelm themselves and end up not knowing what to do next. I could come up with something preachy, but the reality is, you need to know yourself and your limitations. I can learn a ton of things concurrently, contextualize them and isolate them in my mind, but most people can't. If you have a tendency to get overwhelmed by too much information, then just focus on learning the next one or two things you need to move forward.

On a similar note, I shouldn't have to say it because we're all adults here, but I will anyway… Be conscious of your time and your money when it comes to learning about running an online business. I've seen people checking out of their home life or running up tens of thousands in credit card debt "learning". Remember, everything in moderation.

We're always learning in life. To be the best you can be, you need to be a student of the game, you need to get out there and see the good, the bad and the ugly that other people are doing. Most importantly though, you need to take those learnings and apply them to what you're doing because the most important step in learning is application.

Takeaway Item: Think about where you're at with your knowledge base and identify the next one or two things that you need to know to move your online business forward. From there, go do your research and immerse yourself in those topics.

Become An Authority, Experts Are Overrated

Sometimes I like to stir the pot. I just throw out a comment on Facebook to see how people respond. Not too long ago I did this in a group I'm on with some successful Udemy Instructors.

I dropped the following comment:

"An expert is someone who tells other people how much they know about something. An authority is the person other people refer to as experts."

I wanted to see how they'd react because a lot of these people consider themselves "experts" in whatever their chosen field is. The reality is that many of them are experts but I knew the ones that would respond were neither experts or authorities.

I received back a plethora of responses that ranged from weird to the downright silly, but almost every single person that responded underestimated the value of establishing authority. To be fair, most people do and it was what I expecting.

Let me give you a great example - Neil deGrasse Tyson. He's one of the world's leading experts in astrophysics and cosmology, but if that's all he was, you'd probably never have heard of him. There are plenty of incredibly smart astrophysicists and no doubt some of whom are way more accomplished than him, but he's the only one who is hosting a talk show about science on the National Geographic channel.

What he's managed to do is parlay his expertise into authority. When people think about the nature of space and the universe, people immediately think of Neil deGrasse Tyson and Stephen Hawking.

And that's where the money is because that's where the audience lives.

The key to this is "expert positioning". You need to be acknowledged as an expert at something by a broader community. You need to be the "go to person" on your particular topic within a segment of whatever market you're in.

The most effective way to do this is to build your own platform. This is a strategic undertaking that takes time to execute. You'll see this theme of building your own platform mentioned across many of these rules because it is vitally important to your success

On your platform you need to share good quality content or ideas with your community over a period of time that is focused on "the big picture" without diving into the details. If you sell products or services, that's where the detail comes in and your expertise shines through.

You need to extend your reach to other people's platforms to build your authority. Being asked to speak at events and doing guest appearances on other people's podcasts are great examples. You're going to have to start small, it's unlikely that Adam Carolla is going to invite you to be a guest on his podcast next week.

I'm just going to branch out for a second on this topic of appearing on other people's platforms. You need to be a bit tactical about this, so here are some guidelines:

- Do your research about the person and the event or show before you accept. You never want to appear somewhere that doesn't fit with your image;

- Try to find related audiences to yours with minimal overlap, but enough that the audience will be interested;
- When you're starting out, it will be slow going. Once you have some momentum, try to stick to audiences of your size or bigger;
- Entertain people primarily and sprinkle in enough education to demonstrate that you have some expertise;
- Teach people about the outcome, don't show them how to get there, that's why they need to come follow you; and,
- Tell the audience how they can find you.

Again, don't forget to build your own platform, that's a key component. You can start with a simple blog, maybe do some videos if you're comfortable with that, put together your own podcast, write a book and just generally put yourself out there.

Finally, there's no point in having all of this authority unless you have something to sell people. Make sure you take the time to create some products and services that are a logical progression for your audience to buy so that they can tap into your expertise.

Takeaway Item: Becoming an Authority is about being the "go to person" in your market; the person whose opinion is almost definitive about a particular topic. Start building your own platform right away where you can seed high quality content and establish your expertise. Appearing on other people's platforms helps build your authority and your audience as people discover you.

Do One Thing At A Time (and Do It Well)

Ok, show of hands... Put your hand up if you have four or five different projects on the go and you're struggling to get any of them completed.

I know that my hand is up in the air right now (which is making it exceptionally hard to type).

Ok, put your hand down. Now punch yourself in the face because you're limiting your own success. I'm kidding, don't punch yourself. Just feel shame and self-loathing.

The overwhelming majority of people who are even slightly entrepreneurial in nature also have several new ideas on the go at any one time. I could get philosophical or start babbling on using pop psychology ideas, but the reality is, if you're reading this, you can probably relate to what I'm saying.

I'll talk about myself because I created this rule to try and correct this behavior in me. I'm horrible at getting a good idea, starting down the path, making good progress and then getting distracted by some other project or initiative. I often find myself bouncing between several of these ideas at the same time and not making great progress on any of them.

In computer science and programming, this is called Context Switching and Multitasking. Computers are exceptional at this, but humans, not so much.

Let's dive into this a bit more because this is a really good analogy.

When a computer starts working on a problem, it is broken up into a series of calculations and functions that get put in a queue, processed rapidly in order and re-assembled to deliver the output. To switch from one problem to the next is very "cheap" for a computer because it is designed to do this context switching. Modern computers have the ability to work on multiple work queues concurrently which is multitasking.

Conversely, the cost of context switching in the human brain is very high. Our brains are extremely complicated so stopping one task to do the next takes time. More importantly, we have this underlying persistent storage in our brains that we refer to as our subconscious. When you work on multiple things concurrently, your subconscious starts surfacing unrelated problems and your overall efficiency starts taking a dive. If a computer starts introducing fragments of unrelated code from its memory into its processing queue things break and we call that a bug.

The brain is a marvelous thing when you think about it. Mechanically it is running an incredibly complex machine without your conscious mind having to spend one single thought cycle considering it. Blood pressure, blinking your eyes and not drowning in your own spit all happen without you having to even think about it.

But your conscious brain cannot multitask in the truest sense of the word. You cannot think about two things at once. Try it. Think about what you want for dinner and where you parked your car. Your brain will process those two things sequentially for sure and it can do it really, really fast, but it won't process them concurrently.

And those are just two very simple tasks. The projects you are working on are probably a lot more complex and require considerably more thought than where you left your car.

I've come to realize that this disjointed approach to getting things done is really holding me back from reaching my fullest potential. My wife has been saying this for years, but I'm pretty stubborn (or stupid, you decide) and I've only just realized she's right. As a result, I'm going to force myself to live by this rule in 2016 - do one thing at a time, finish things, simplify and do less, but do it better.

I actually started this process in mid-November 2015 when the Casual Marketer project started taking shape in my mind. I realized that this was something that I wanted to do starting in January 2016, so I spent most of November just closing off old projects in my own mind. I was quietly reviewing everything I had on the go and coming to terms with putting it on the backburner or shutting it down altogether in 2016.

And that's when the magic started happening. By closing off the things I didn't want to do, my focus and brain power started shifting to the one project I wanted to do. Every spare thought cycle I had my mind would gravitate towards solving some problem or crafting a new idea about the Newsletter project. Nothing else polluted my thinking because I'd decided fundamentally to focus on this project.

Which leads us to this book. I had the idea pop into my head in early November, but I shelved it after collecting the rules and writing them down in a Google Doc. By early December I'd pretty much worked out how I was going to put together the newsletter and the business model. I decided that I wanted the book to be part of the offer. So rather than wasting time creating web pages, optin forms, setting up order pages, I put all of that aside, started writing this book and made amazing progress very quickly.

I'm entirely confident that this type of focus is going to really change me because I can already see the results in this one project. You can do this too. Just take a half day, sit down with a notepad and write down all of the projects you are working on. Then go through them. Be brutal. Identify which things are not going to move the needle for you and are just a distraction, then figure out how to kill them off.

Everything that's left goes into your processing queue and doesn't get worked on until the previous task is done or you've decided to kill it off. No exceptions, you have to be ruthless especially if you have a job or other substantial commitments like your family or a hobby you're heavily involved in.

This has been a revelation for me, and it will be for you too!

Takeaway Item: Cut out the distractions especially the projects that aren't part of your core business. By focusing more on fewer things, your quality and speed of execution will increase.

Section 2

THE "DON'T" RULES

Don't Be A Digital Sharecropper

If the rule, "You're In The Traffic Business" is the one that kickstarted the process of this book, then it was this rule that ignited the fire in me to not only get this book done, but to also launch the whole Casual Marketer idea!

As I've said earlier in the introduction, I've been doing online marketing for a relatively long time in the grand scheme of things and I've acquired a fair bit of knowledge. I also like teaching people and working with them to improve their businesses both offline and online. As a result, when you put these things together with the fact that I'm a fairly technical individual, it only makes sense that I'd gravitate towards creating online courses and information products.

Over the years I've created numerous online training programs and for the most part I've self-hosted them and drove my own traffic either directly or by working with partners and affiliates. Back in late 2012, I created a course that walked people through how to create and run their own podcast, it was called

RapidAction Podcasting. It did pretty well, it sold over 1500 copies in the ten-day launch window, plus about 40% of customers took the extended version at a higher price point.

After the launch my wife suggested that I try posting it on this new platform she'd come across called Udemy. I wasn't really interested as I'd just had a successful launch and a week later I was starting a new job that I was pretty excited about. We agreed that I would create a Udemy instructor profile, link it to my PayPal account but she would upload the course and set the whole thing up.

We did that and I promptly forgot about Udemy. I got stuck into my job and at the same time our other online business activities were ticking over so Udemy never really made an impact with us.

Fast forward to the first week of August 2014 and I noticed that I got this $50 PayPal deposit in an account I hardly ever used. I logged into the PayPal account and it had about $500 in it. I went back looked at the email and it was from Udemy. How random.

After piecing this all together I logged into Udemy and had a look around. Every month for about eighteen months they'd been sending me between $20 and $50. I was quite literally doing nothing for this money, I didn't even know it was there.

Looking around Udemy I started to notice that there were plenty of people apparently selling a ton of digital courses. I spent the next month or so buying the odd Udemy course, hanging around their Facebook group and trying to figure out what was going on.

By mid-October 2014 I'd decided I wanted to give Udemy a shot, so I put together my "Easy SEO For Wordpress" course. I stupidly launched it after the start of the big Black Friday promotion so I totally missed out on that but even still, without doing anything at all my little course started selling.

And it kept on selling. December's revenue beat November's. January 2015 beat December. February beat January. On and on this went for months.

I put together a quick business plan in early January for my Udemy efforts with some pretty aggressive projections and started thinking of new course ideas. Over the next few months

I released a Wordpress Security course which did well and helped take my revenue higher again.

Then reality started to set in for me around May 2015. Udemy were beta testing some new layouts and I could see that these were going to have a big effect. From the initial beta release I could see that this wasn't going to be good for me. I had one more course in the pipeline I was working on, but I decided to maybe put a hold on spending more time on creating Udemy courses.

It wasn't just the layout change to be honest, it was a confluence of events. There were people in the marketplace cheating pretty significantly and going unpunished, I wasn't seeing any of my students joining my own email lists and Udemy were starting to talk about instructors promoting their own courses BEFORE they would start seeing some organic Udemy traffic.

I quickly realized that I'd broken one of my own rules that I'd had for a number of years, "Don't Be A Digital Sharecropper". I'd allowed myself to become a tenant on Udemy's land, tilling their soil, fixing their plant and machinery while giving them the power at any time to change the terms of our deal to slant the odds in their favor even more.

I was stupid and I knew it. That hurt.

June was a record revenue month for me on Udemy, but in the third week of that month they formally introduced the new layouts. July saw a 40% decline in revenue and traffic had plummeted. By August my revenue was down 60% from the height of June. At the time of writing this chapter my December revenues are trending about 10% of June and about 30% of last December when I had really just gotten started seriously.

Luckily, the Udemy income for me isn't that significant and the lesson was more one of frustration because I knew better! I was allowing my content and effort to be housed on someone else's platform that was allowing them to build their business while giving me crumbs. I've seen people with five and six figure per month Facebook Groups closed down without notice in the last two years, so it could have been much worse!

With your business online, you need to be independent and in control of your own success and failure. Your business needs to not be at the whim of someone else's decisions or actions based on their selfish motives. Setup a self-hosted Wordpress site, start building an email list, do a podcast, get PayPal and Stripe payment processing accounts.

Own the land you intend to farm on because nobody can ever take that away from you or change the rules in such a way that it damages your business significantly.

There's nothing wrong with having a Udemy course or posting YouTube videos, just make sure that at the end of the day, everything points people back to the web property that you own.

Takeaway Item: Be the master of your own domain! Everything you do online should be about establishing your own authority, building your assets and protecting your business. Don't waste your time building someone else's business for table scraps.

Don't Be The Conductor Of The Free Train!

Choo! Choo! All aboard! The free train is pulling out of the station, next stop, Loserville.

I myself have been guilty of giving away too much valuable information for free. Sometimes you don't even know you're doing it, you're just talking to someone, they're asking a few questions and BOOM, you're not only telling people where the gold is buried, you're drawing them a map and offering to carry their shovel for them.

I've put the brakes on this behavior. It's taken a bit of a mindset shift for sure. I have to catch myself before I start talking.

It almost always starts with, "Hey Sean, I wanted to pick your brain…"

When I first realized that that phrase was going to lead to the person saying they wanted something for free, I began to physically pinch my hand out of their field of vision. It sounds silly, but I thought that if I could create a Pavlovian pain response to that phrase that I'd be less inclined to engage.

I didn't need to go to that extreme to be honest, the reality is, just acknowledging it and feeling the need to get out of that horrific pattern of behavior was probably enough.

Now if someone sends me an email seeking free advice, I usually just tell them the end result without telling them the "how".

Why is that important? Because it's almost useless to them. They need to come back with asking how do they achieve that. Most people realize at this point they are stretching the friendship, but every so often, some clueless person doesn't, so I politely but firmly tell them that my time costs $250 per hour and if they're interested in booking some time then we can try and coordinate our schedules.

Some people can take offense to this, but that's because they've "friend zoned" you. They don't look at you like an authority or even an expert. They see you as a mate. That's bad for business. Your time and your knowledge are valuable, you shouldn't be expected to give it away for free!

And the problem is, as I've learned the hard way over the years, people value your time directly proportional to the amount they pay for it. If someone "picks your brain" for free, there's a better than average chance they will do absolutely nothing with that information.

You see this all the time in business, a staff member makes a suggestion and it gets ignored, but when a high priced consultant makes the same suggestion suddenly it's the best idea since sliced bread. It's stupid, but it's the truth.

Another impact to you is that if you're the "free advice" person, then the overall perceived value of you and what you do is diminished.

Ok, let's unpack that that statement a bit.

It doesn't mean people don't respect you or they don't think you're smart, it's just market dynamics. If you are free and loose with your advice, then it becomes easy to get and less rare. When something is abundant and readily available, it becomes less valuable, that's just the way markets work.

And the devaluation is like a cancer, it spreads. People will start to think your time isn't worth much so everything else you do suddenly becomes cheapened.

The other piece to bear in mind is curiosity.

Curiosity is one of the best tools you can use from a selling perspective, people just need to know what's behind door number two. When you're someone that people respect and admire as having a certain level of expertise then by not giving away too much free advice, you trigger curiosity in people. And they'll pay to find out what you know!

Takeaway Item: Don't be the person who gives away too much free advice because you'll end up just devaluing yourself and your business in general.

Don't Be Homer

If I were a different person, I'd sit down and write a whole business book about how to succeed in business by watching Homer J Simpson, patriarch of TV's Simpson family. Homer gives us so many business lessons from his failures, that realistically, most MBA programs would be better off just handing students a DVD collection of the Simpsons.

Yes, I just suggested using DVDs. Next chapter will all be about programming the time on your VCR and how to manually rewind an 8-track tape.

There are a couple classic Homer lessons, that I want to share.

Marge goes to an Investorettes meeting and feeling inspired decides to go into business for herself so she starts making pretzels. She has some initial success but then things slow down, so Homer decides that she needs to "think bigger" and scale up so he cuts a deal with local mob boss, Fat Tony, to do distribution. His deal with Fat Tony entitles the mob to 100% of her profits.

This is affiliate marketing in a nutshell. Not all affiliate marketing is bad, but a lot of it is. You lose control of your distribution, you end up having to support the business and generally a large portion of your profit walks out the door to someone who may or may not be representing you in the marketplace the way you want to be represented.

I like affiliate marketing and if done well, it can really turbocharge your business, but if you go into it like Homer from a position of weakness, then you're in trouble. Luckily for Marge when the mob turned up on her doorstep looking to collect their "pretzel monies" the Investorettes had the Yakuza to call on to help her out. You unfortunately won't have the Yakuza to protect you from dodgy affiliates.

Don't be Homer.

In another episode, Homer's long lost brother Herb (voiced by Danny DeVito) is a successful, rich, car manufacturing champion of industry. Herb thinks that Homer is in touch with the common man, people that Herb's management drones don't relate to at all.

Herb decides to roll the dice and let Homer design a car.

Homer starts off the design process getting bullied by the engineers who want him to have "Rack and Peanut steering". Herb inspires Homer to find his voice. Hilarity ensues.

Ultimately, Homer designs a car that is hideously ugly, stupidly impractical, has a multitude of cup holders (you can never have enough cup holders) and the most important feature is the horn plays "La Cucaracha". The car has a sticker price of $82,000. And with that, Herb's company is ruined and goes bankrupt.

The lesson here is pretty simple, designing your product or service to suit your tastes is often a very poor idea. One of our other rules talks about knowing your market and part of that is not confusing what you like, with what they need. I see so many people creating solutions for problems that nobody has that it's embarrassing. Listen to your market, understand their pain, solve their problem, take your own bias out of the equation as much as possible.

Don't be Homer.

The last example I'm going to give is from a classic Simpson's episode called "Das Bus". Homer discovers that his neighbor and nemesis, Ned Flanders has started his own home-based business on the internet called Flancrest Enterprises. Homer decides to setup "Compu-Global-Hyper-Mega-Net" that is effectively just a web page with a hit counter on it. Homer even automates his metrics reporting by getting a little mechanical bird to tap the refresh key so he can see how many visits he has.

Homer eventually gets bought out by Bill Gates. And by bought out I mean Gates turns up to the Simpson house with his goons, smashes Homer's computer and home office. Gates tells Homer that he didn't get rich by writing cheques.

There are so many small lessons in this episode about online business that it's like a masterclass. Copying people online is a plague. I learn the most from watching the mistakes that other people make, I see something and I say, "Wow, there's some ninja level failure right there, don't make that mistake." The overwhelming majority of people doing business online end up just copying the mistakes. The expert copiers are often the people who tactically pick the mistakes from a wide range of people and stitch them together to make an absolute mistake bomb.

Then there is the idea of tracking the wrong metrics. I've heard "hits" referred to as "How Idiots Track Success" and that sums it up. Most people in business look at the wrong metrics. You need to figure out which are the important numbers and keep a close eye on those. More importantly, figure out the metrics around those numbers that can give you some future looking indicators of how those numbers might be trending. Let me give you a quick clue, "Net Profit" is a great number to look at.

Finally, I mentioned Homer having the little bird tapping the refresh button to display his "hit counter" for him. I see this all the time and I call it "Automating Stupidity". People spend an inordinate amount of time figuring out how to automate the most useless tasks. Why? Most of the effort is to automate something you shouldn't be doing anyway. People get carried away with automation sometimes and they convince themselves it will be a huge time saver.

Don't be Homer.

Takeaway Item: I'll say it again, Don't Be Homer! Seriously though, if you find yourself emulating a cartoon character that is intentionally written to be a buffoon, you may have a problem. Focus on customer problems, delivering value and tracking the right things in your business.

Don't Get Caught Buying Hope

The number one easiest thing to sell on the internet is, wait for it… Hope.

I'm a pretty keen observer of how people market themselves and what they offer potential customers. A few years ago most internet marketing gurus were selling you knowledge about how to do something specific that would accelerate what you were doing and take you into the stratosphere financially.

Of course, most of it was crap and very quickly people started to realize the results they were suggesting were impossible to achieve. The idea that someone could teach you some mechanics around a funnel or list building that would allow you to press the "interwebz monies magic button" whenever you wanted and you'd become rich is ludicrous.

More importantly though, it's a flawed business model, but probably not for the reason you think.

Selling knowledge is actually pretty important. I mean at the heart of this book, my Casual Marketer Monthly Newsletter and my coaching programs, I'm selling knowledge. It would be hypocritical to suggest that the internet marketing gurus were full of crap and somehow what I'm offering doesn't stink as well.

No, the problem has nothing to do with the actual knowledge because in some cases it was pretty good stuff. The flaw in the business model was actually with the customer!

Yep, you heard that right - the buyer was the problem. Let me explain.

The vast majority of people that buy information products do absolutely nothing with them. They are either collectors or they are lazy and in some cases, probably both. I can see on some platforms that as much as 80% of the people who buy my training products never even look at them. Another 10% might look at five minutes of video or less. These folks seem to get a rush out of buying and that fulfills their need for a period of time.

The rest of your customers, the 10% or so who actually consume the content again fall into two broad groups: one group that takes that knowledge and apply it; and, a second group that takes the knowledge and rationalizes to themselves why it won't apply to them. Let's say that these two groups are 5% each.

Ok, let's break that first group down one more time. These are the 5% of people who take what's being taught and try to apply it. Right off the bat I can tell you that most of these people will straight up try to copy it almost verbatim and they will fail. Without being overly harsh, these people are too stupid to innovate even a tiny bit. They are persistent and dogged, but they just don't have the overall intelligence required to succeed.

Which leaves us with 1% or 2% of all customers who buy information products and take full advantage of them. The best gurus turn these people into case studies and testimonials to convince future buyers of how invaluable this information is. That's just good marketing to be blunt.

If this were the end of our story, we'd say it was just a numbers game and move on. You now have 99% of your audience that aren't being successful and as I've outlined above, it is largely their own fault.

But even that's not the problem!

The problem is that the 99% will almost certainly never take personal responsibility for their own failings. They will blame the seller. The seller is at fault for them being a collector or for not being smart enough to implement what they were taught.

It's just human nature. The vast majority of us lack the self-awareness to be introspective enough to work out why we don't succeed. We externalize and move on because it diverts the spotlight away from our own weakness. It's just easier to deal with.

And therein lies the big internet marketing guru problem - the quality of the knowledge they were providing was largely irrelevant because the overwhelming majority of customers were simply never going to succeed and were going to blame them for their failure. And for the most part, that's what happened.

For the smarter ones the answer was pretty simple, stop selling results and start selling hope. Hope doesn't fail, it just hasn't been realized yet. Hope requires no real tangible outcome. Most importantly, for the gurus it completely flips the math around. All of the things that end up leading to the 99% of customer failing are virtually irrelevant and best of all, their failure can be assuaged with a healthy dose of more hope. For the 1% who previously were successful, who cares. They'll probably be successful no matter what. They're alpha human beings. For the gurus, the other 99% is where the money is.

So why am I sharing this with you and what's the point of this rule?

First of all, I'm telling you this so you'll be aware. If someone starts showing you their flash car, taking pictures of their big house and telling you they only work five hours a week from the beach because they've figured it out, they are selling you hope. They are banking on the fact that you probably feel that you're as smart as them and you want to barely work while going on seemingly endless vacations.

Secondly, in whatever you do in your online business activities, don't sell people hope. You can sell positivity and share your successes by all means, but don't try and gloss over the effort required to be successful. Be honest and ethical!

Takeaway Item: If someone spends more time trying to sell you their lifestyle without sharing the hard work required to get it, they're selling you a big bag of hope. Focus on outcomes and be honest with people you deal with and yourself!

Section 3

The Intimate Relationship Between Sales and Delivery

Nothing Happens Until Someone Sells Something

It almost seems ridiculous that if you consider yourself to be in business, that you actually need a reminder to "sell" stuff, but the reality is, for many people selling doesn't come naturally or worse, you may even dislike selling.

My friend James Schramko has a saying that I've heard him use a few times, but the most memorable was this one time on stage where he was speaking to about 100 people and the audience nodded so much I thought there may long term neck damage for some of them. James says, "People only buy things to be better off. A sale is the process of change from one situation to a BETTER alternative situation."

I think that's really profound. We buy things because we value what we're buying MORE than the money it costs to buy it. Most of us place an inherent, but somewhat fluid value on money. When we have less money, we value it more. When we have a tough job, we appreciate the money we get paid more. Conversely, when you have plenty of money, you can be a bit more frivolous and things we "want" become more important than money so we end up buying more.

But at the heart of it all is a sale. You don't really have a business until you're selling something.

And for many people running their own online business, they would say that selling is the hardest thing they have to do.

I think it's actually more of a perception and confidence issue. When we think of selling, our mind conjures up this notion of some shifty character trying to trick us out of our money. We immediately think of a used car salesmen or some street hustler selling knock off Rolex watches.

But that's not really what selling is, you don't have to be those people.

I openly admit that I've always struggled with this myself and this rule is probably the first one that I informally created to get over that problem. It was so ironic because while I struggled with the idea of selling, everyone I came across would say, "You're really good at selling." I would thank them and in my mind I'd be replaying conversations to weed out where they thought I was trying to sell something to them because I figured I must have been coming across as disingenuous.

About three years ago it dawned on me, I was always selling. Not in some douchey, disingenuous way, but by actually listening to people, understanding their problem and trying to help them. I was subconsciously positioning myself as the conduit to the "better alternative situation" for that person in a genuine way. And I never realized I was actually doing it.

For me, this was a monumental shift in my thinking. I went from having a distaste for selling to actually enjoying the whole process. It was pretty invigorating.

I then realized that while my "style" of selling resonated with people, I was actually doing them a massive disservice at the same time. I wasn't making them an offer. I was demonstrating that I could help them with their problem, but I wasn't telling them how to take to take the next step. I was putting this other person in a position where they would have to ask not only for my help, but how they could give me money for it. How uncomfortable is that?

I'm still working on the making offers part. That doesn't really come naturally for me and it's something that I openly admit that I'm trying to learn how to drop it into conversations so that it comes across as cool. I'm getting better at it, but I've still got a way to go.

And that's what I want this rule to do for you! I want you to realize that you have to sell and that by making well placed, well considered offers you are actually helping people. You're giving them an option to work with you to help them achieve that "better alternative situation".

Think about your online business from the perspective of:

Demonstrating value to people;
Addressing the problems of your intended audience; and,
Making them an offer that helps them get to their outcome.

That is the basis of selling, it really isn't that hard and it works for everything. It can be content marketing, presenting to an audience from stage or in emails to your list. It really is that simple – provide value then make an offer.

Takeaway Item: Think about what you do online and in your interactions with customers. Are you following up with an actual offer? Selling isn't about tricking people out of their money, it's about helping customers and clients improve their situation through buying what you offer.

Thou Shalt Know Thy Market

Bad marketing sticks out like a sore thumb and probably the most revolting form of marketing is when the person doesn't really understand the market they are pitching. Immediately the person looks like an amateur and that lack of understanding becomes a massive sales inhibitor.

The best way of course to know and understand your market is to actually be part of it! If you're participating in the conversation with your intended audience, not only are you building authority (which is critical) but you're also learning what the market wants, needs and responds to. By being a member of this community you're learning the landscape, the language and the customs of the people you want to sell to. As a result, when it comes time to make your offer, it will be familiar and assuming your copy is even passable, it will resonate.

A few years back I went through the process of having my sleep examined by doctors. I was struggling to stay awake, my snoring had reached levels where my wife was putting in earplugs in the next room and overall I just felt like crap most of the time. I knew I had sleep apnea, but I didn't really know too much about it.

I went to the specialist and did the overnight sleep survey at the hospital. My score for measuring apnea events was really high, literally more than once a minute my breathing would stop over the course of a night. During the entire night of the study, eight hours sleep, I never entered the deepest levels of REM sleep - to give you some perspective, that type of sleep deprivation is a form of torture banned by the Geneva Conventions.

I got the report a week later from the doctor and started doing research. I found entire sleep apnea communities online. I immersed myself in the literature available. When it came time to get my CPAP machine and mask, I rented just about every type available and tried them all out. I learned everything I could about the equipment and the problem itself.

And then I started sharing it in forums and I even created a blog talking about my own experiences. Three years later that blog still ranks highly in Google for a bunch of good keywords, gets traffic and I get at least one question via the site every week. People would send me emails and ask me if I sold CPAP equipment so they could buy from me because I helped them so much.

It doesn't take long to become part of a community and to learn a market, especially if you're interested in it. I have always admired the top copywriters who can study a market from a distance, learn the nuances, understand the market's pain and then write compelling copy around that. For some people, it's like a gift and just comes naturally, but that doesn't mean you can't develop that knowledge and skill set with some effort and time.

The key thing is understanding the pain points the market has. What I did with sleep apnea was recognize that the number one problem people had was finding a CPAP mask that didn't irritate them when they slept. I was lucky, I had no trouble with every single mask I tried, but some people really struggle. I tried them all and I wrote about them for people. I was like their crash test dummy of CPAP masks. More importantly, when I would write about masks, I knew their pain and I knew the product so it made it easy to write.

There's the old copywriting truism that says you sell benefits, not features. The big step that you can take when you understand the pain points of your market is being able to position what you're offering as a benefit that relieves their pain point. People buy pain relief when they have a headache, they don't buy "headache prevention pills" when they are perfectly ok. Knowing your market makes that messaging so much more genuine and smooth.

When you get these things wrong though, it can be a train wreck. I saw one of the best examples of this with someone who created a Udemy course in mid-2015. This guy created a course about "How to make a Udemy course in under six hours". There were so many problems:

- First of all, it was the first Udemy course he'd ever created. He was teaching something he'd never done before;
- He was promoting this course in a community of existing Udemy instructors where he had never posted anything, so nobody knew who he was and he had zero authority; and,
- He completely misunderstood the pain most of the audience had so his main selling point didn't solve a real problem.

It was farcical and easily one of the worst efforts I'd seen in a long time. He wasn't part of the community, he didn't really understand the market he was trying to serve and he made an offer that was incongruent with the pain his intended audience had. It was like a trifecta of terrible.

Before you go into a market, just set aside a set period of time to not only research it, but if there are active communities out there, join them. Take part in the conversation. The Cluetrain Manifesto said that with the internet revolution, markets are conversations. I totally agree with this. Customers are using the power of the internet to congregate and coalesce around solutions to their problems. The best companies are the one that participate in that conversation as equals, giving as much as they get. You want to be one of those companies.

Takeaway Item: Knowing your market is vital to your success. If you know what pain people are having it becomes easier to serve them. Participating in your market's community will give you greater insight and help you establish authority.

Attract Ideal Customers, Repel Everybody Else

One of the worst mistakes you can make in running your online business is thinking that what you offer can serve everyone or that you can solve everybody's problem. Without having properly identified your perfect customer with the problem you are best qualified to help them solve, you're starting from a place of poor focus.

Almost everyone I know who's had any kind of level of success from running an online business has almost always had a few false starts. Normally, these are the result of not having a deep enough understanding of your market or what your own value proposition is and that ends up with you attracting the wrong leads and customers.

I've made this mistake a few times in my own online businesses.

A couple years back I spent some time targeting people in the Internet Marketing world. Creating products targeted at the Warrior Forum user base was entirely incongruent with my personality and way of doing business. Most of those people were just interested in superficial information or the latest "push button money making" solution, they weren't really interested in learning something in a meaningful way and applying it.

Now with that said, I had some success in that space. I created a couple products that people bought and made some money, but the reality was that it wasn't a market that was attractive to me. There are plenty of people who still make a ton of money targeting those people, but it wasn't a fit for the way I do things. The people who are successful there are constantly launching new products and bouncing from one thing to the next. I'm more inclined to focus on something and try to master it. That market doesn't appreciate mastery.

Similarly, when we started our RapidAction Writing business we built up a client base quickly of people who were doing low cost white-labelling of our content. It generated quite a bit of initial work for that business and the associated income, but there was also a big disconnect. Our content was properly researched, well written and took time to create. This was incongruent with some of our bigger customers because they were interested in fast turnarounds with very keyword dense articles and quality was secondary. As a result, we ended up having a disconnect on price and volume

In both of these instances, I could have had success by just changing what I did to suit the market, but honestly, that's not a great way forward. I'm not saying you shouldn't change to meet market conditions sometimes, but if you are running a steak restaurant, your ideal customers are probably not vegetarians.

Being able to make this distinction requires some self-awareness and some confidence in what you're doing. You need to have done the introspective reflection to know who you're most likely to be able to help but also be sure enough of your own abilities to say "NO" to leads that aren't right for you. When you're starting out, this can be hard, so don't be too tough on yourself if you've compromised a bit, just know that to eventually have the success you want, you will have to fix that.

There are a few key elements to making this rule work for you:

- You need to be able to attract these people, so you need to know where they are online or how you can get in front of them;

- You must understand what makes them unique as a group that you can target; and,
- You have to make it abundantly clear who your offer is not well suited for.

The first two are basic market research principles and we cover that in the rule about knowing your market, so there's no point going into it here. It goes without saying that you need to know who your ideal customer is before you can target them.

The repelling part is a bit trickier. You can be very overt or quite subtle in how you do this and to be 100% honest with you, it can be a bit fluid. For example, in our writing business, we expressly say that we DO NOT write content on topics like SEO or internet marketing. That eliminates a bunch of people we don't want to work with straightaway and that's pretty overt.

On the other hand, while our ideal market isn't people who are white-labelling our work, under the right circumstances, we can work well with people like this and some of our best customers in that business operate this way. To subtly eliminate many of these type of customers, we have a price point that would be expensive for them to stick a margin on top of and resell to their customers. Basically, our price point effectively eliminates the people we least like dealing with, the people who want cheap and nasty content.

The last point I'd make about this rule is that you have to avoid classifying "anyone who can pay" as your ideal customer. You see this happen when people get desperate and candidly, it's very hard to avoid. You need to think bigger picture and be patient when the urge to "just take the money" arises because in the long term, it will hurt you more than it helps.

Takeaway Item: You will be most happy and do your best work if you are working with your ideal customers. You need to be very clear about who you can best serve, but also who you're not suited to work with. Price and delivery methodologies are great ways to exclude people you're not suited to working with.

Referrals: The Second Most Powerful Force In The Universe

There's the old adage that the most powerful force in the known universe is compound interest. For people who've had credit card debt at 19% compound interest, I'd venture a guess and say that they probably would agree with this statement unequivocally.

But for me, in how I've run various businesses online over the years, there's almost nothing as powerful as customer referrals. In fact, about 80% of all the money I've ever made online in my own services businesses have come from referrals. I've done almost zero paid advertising and sporadic content marketing. I'm reasonably good at managing relationships, but again, those usually come from referrals.

Referrals are the centerpiece of my online services business.

And that's not by luck, but by design which is an important distinction to remember.

Gaining referrals is a process that needs to define your entire customer lifecycle. Once someone has heard about you for the first time (ideally from an existing customer), all the way through the feeling out phase, the purchase and post-sale, everything should be tailored to ensuring that customer will want to tell their friends, colleagues and neighbors about you and your business.

Referrals are actually a fundamental part of the human psyche. When we spend money on something, we're taking a risk. Often times people we know and those who are close to us are aware of the risk. When that risk pays off and we get a good outcome, we want to tell them that it went well for us and as a result two things happen: one, we slightly embellish the results to increase their approval of us; and two, we want them to confirm our choice by them buying too.

It goes even further and deeper than this and you probably see it happen all the time without even noticing it. When someone tells a group of people about a problem or need they have, immediately people chime in with a referral - someone always "knows a guy". By telling people about our success we gain esteem in their eyes but we also feel even better about our own choice. It elevates us within that social group.

And that's just the emotional and psychology need for us to actually make referrals, there's also the aspect of being the person who's just been given a referral. Being able to send an email to someone you don't know and say, "Hi, Jeff said you were the guy to talk to about SEO" has an array of psychological elements to it as well!

By telling someone that you've been referred we're subconsciously fulfilling a couple of our own needs. We're removing some risk for ourselves with reaching out to establish a new relationship because the referral gives us the upper hand, "I know what you do because Jeff told me" and it also creates a familiarity to someone you have no working history with. Getting a referral puts us at a greater sense of ease which makes buying easier.

The key for you is, don't screw up with the referred business! You need to deliver the goods to the person who's been referred to you. If you make a mess you can really hurt your business because first of all, you've done a bad job for a customer, but secondly, that person will tell the customer who referred them and now you've potentially poisoned two relationships. Keep that in mind!

I've seen people try and build all kinds of elaborate reward systems and kickbacks for customers who send referrals, but this isn't something that I've ever bothered with. I personally, just call them and say "Thanks" or mention it the next time I see them.

If you go back, I talked about processes around getting referrals. I didn't say gimmicks. You should be building out your business to deliver people excellent results and "delight" them with your customer service. Those two things are the most important aspects of getting referrals.

Takeaway Item: People want to tell other people they know about good experiences they have with service providers. It's a mutually beneficial outcome. You get the immediate accrual of trust predicated on someone else's relationship and they get to bask in the glow of your good work for the person they referred. The key to all of this is delivering a product or service that is "referral worthy."

Under Promise and Over Deliver

Too many times you see things online that with any kind of clarity of thought you'd realize were too good to be true. It happens all the time, people get wrapped up in the hype of a product launch or the sweet siren song of a well written sales letter.

But neither of these things really get my goat as much as people who fail to deliver on what they promise.

One of my worst experiences with online and internet marketing was back in 2011 when a couple of "big hitters" were launching their own link tracking software targeted at people doing paid traffic like cost-per-view and pay-per-view. This product was priced at $1997 and for an additional $97/mth you could be part of their weekly webinar mastermind program where they promised to show you their traffic sources, landing pages and how they were not only using the tool, but how they were making money in that market.

I ended up getting the product for free as a successful affiliate in an effort by them to get me to try and promote it. The tool itself was actually pretty good software, reasonably well written and largely did what they promised. I was impressed.

Based on that I decided to try out their mastermind group, so I plunked down my $97 for the first month and signed up for the first webinar. That's where my disappointment began.

The two founders who were meant to be running the webinar turned up late, didn't really have anything lined up to present and pretty much wasted everyone's time, let alone money. I sent them an email and told them it appeared they didn't really know much about the market they were serving. I also made the mistake of mentioning a campaign I was testing with their tool.

The next week they asked me if I could run the webinar… Long story short within a few weeks they just walked away and I was now running their mastermind.

If that was the end of the story, that would be bad, but it gets worse.

Everyone who bought the product got a free ticket to their two-day live event in San Diego. The first day was ok, but one of the two guys behind the product disappeared midway through the day. He turned up that night at the "VIP Dinner" where people had paid $1000 to eat with the speakers, but clearly he was as the Aussies say, "tired and emotional."

That founder didn't even turn up on the second day... And of course, he was presenting two of the sessions. The other founder tried to improvise but we ended up with one session presented by a lady who went into extreme detail about her sex life for most of her 45 minute session and another session where some woman started singing a woo-woo song about being a "magnet for money".

Needless to say, it was farcical.

While it was hilariously funny to me because it really cost me nothing financially, it was the single biggest example of internet marketers not living up to their promises that I'd ever seen.

But the thing is, you never have to do this and it is actually in your best interest to turn that around; you should under promise and over deliver!

Some people are so worried about "making the sale" that they just go too far. They can't possibly ever deliver on the promises they've made let alone the expectations of their buyers and clients.

Over the long haul, you will make more money by honing in on a few key things that you know you can deliver exceptionally well and all of the extra stuff is effectively a bonus for the buyer. They'll be delighted that you've delivered on your core promises at a very high level and they'll be anxious to share with other people the extra stuff you've given them.

In fact, it's really simple human psychology. Everyone wants to feel like they've gotten a great deal and made a good decision when they take a risk and buy something. More importantly, they'll be compelled to tell other people about it because it compounds the psychological benefit.

You know what that is, right? It's the second most powerful force in the universe, a customer referral!

Takeaway Item: By under promising and over delivering you will delight your customers. Delighted customers have a psychological desire to share their experiences with people they respect thus driving referral business to you!

People Will Buy Good Experience

It's the holiday season and there are literally millions of people travelling somewhere to visit friends, family or just go on a short vacation. I was talking to a friend last week and she mentioned that she taking a short trip to Bali to get some rest and relaxation before cracking into the New Year. When I asked if she was excited about the trip, she said she was looking forward to being in Bali, but the whole trip was not something she was looking forward to.

And that's a common experience. When you see surveys about experiences people have the most distaste for, air travel has become one of the worst, finishing just ahead of "visiting the dentist" and "jury duty". In fact, people rated air travel as a worse experience than paying their taxes!

How did this happen? It's a well documented phenomenon that twenty years ago, people actually liked air travel and saw the trip itself as part of the fun of going on vacation. Now though, people absolutely hate it.

The easy answer, which is wrong and lazy, is that the increased focus on security has made the whole process of catching a plane a bit tedious. The truth is, that part of the trip is actually just inconvenient and can be annoying. The real problem is the whole experience of dealing with an airline.

I once had a senior executive of a major international airline in conversation with me jokingly refer to economy class passengers as "self-loading cargo". Apparently this was the joke among airline executives. He even said Premium Economy class seats were refurbished leftovers from the 1990's economy class meaning that the bigger size was actually normal twenty years back.

Now, we see air travel as a necessary evil of going somewhere. Our brand loyalty has disappeared and most of us are willing to travel on the cheapest flights available because the airlines have made us dislike them and their service.

Think about this in your own business because doing a good job matters. Focusing on delivering high levels of customer service engenders loyalty, trust and repeat business. We talked about the power of referrals in this book already, nothing will drive referrals faster than good customer service.

One of the things I'm doing throughout the execution of Casual Marketer is thinking about the entire customer experience from start to finish. I want the entire lifecycle from lead through to long term customer to be an experience that they'd recommend to their friends and family.

To deliver that type of experience you need to think holistically about the process and really put some thought into your onboarding so that people feel engaged and appreciated right away.

As a customer, I'm a really big fan of great onboarding. I think it is one of the most important and often poorly done things not in just online businesses, but in businesses in general. Good onboarding at its core is about helping the customer hit the ground running. You want to help them find a quick win and get immediate value from the product or service they've purchased from you. This obviously serves their purpose of having success, but it also validates their decision to do business with you which is obviously important.

But not everything will work flawlessly and one valuable lesson I've learned over the years of doing online business is the importance of having a good ticketing or help desk system. This book isn't about systems or technology, but I do want to share this story because I think it teaches a really important lesson.

About five years ago I started using Zendesk in my online business. Coming from an Enterprise IT background it worked like a really simple ticketing system that I knew and understood. This went on for about three years and I have to say, I had numerous customers comment that they found the whole support system "hard".

I was talking to a client one day and she said, "I wish your ticket system was just email, it would be so much easier." That made me realize that I was looking at it the wrong way around. I was using my ticketing system to track a bunch of stuff that didn't directly improve customer experience, in fact it damaged it.

Within a few days I'd switched to Help Scout which handles help requests like email. It doesn't have all the reporting and features of Zendesk, but customers who used it really liked it.

One even said it was a relief just to be able to send us emails rather than use a help desk - they were of course still using a ticketing system, we just modified the experience to be easier.

The other thing that happened was that the people who answer my tickets started to shine. They are customer focused and they want to help people. That customer centric approach got lost behind a veneer of crappy software. Immediately people started commenting about how great my team were and then they started telling other people.

Rather than a function that sat in the background when something was wrong, customer support and service moved closer to the clients and became part of the positive experience people have when dealing with us!

It just seems crazy to have to write it down but it's true, every time you interact with a customer is a sales opportunity. Even when something isn't working correctly, by handling it really well and behaving like human beings behave, you're re-affirming in that client's mind that your business is worth doing business with.

Takeaway Item: People are always willing to pay more for good quality. Sometimes "more" could mean the actual price is higher and other times "more" can mean that they are willing to stay with you longer, bringing in repeat business and referrals. Either way, it's easier to have long term success when you deliver a great product or service consistently.

Section 4

Rules for Business Builders

The Marketing Law Of Levers

Throughout this book, I've referred to the lie that everyone tells about content marketing, but in this chapter, I want to explain to you how it can work properly!

Engineering is a fascinating discipline. Great engineers do complex things to achieve monumental outcomes while striving for absolute simplicity.

I'm going to channel the ghost of Archimedes to apply the law of levers to your content marketing.

With leverage there are a few aspects we need to understand:

Load - the thing we're trying to move
Lever - the thing we're trying to use to move the load
Fulcrum - the thing that gives purchase to the lever to gain mechanical advantage
Force - the effort you apply to the lever to move the load

When we speak of "load" in the context of this discussion, what we're talking about is moving your prospects, leads and audience towards making a purchasing decision. This is the movement we're ultimately aiming for and everything else, the lever, the fulcrum and the force are all totally focused on delivering that outcome. Keep that in mind.

Force is another relatively easy thing to describe in this because it's the amount of effort you need to apply to get people to buy. I like to think of force in this sense as sales tactics, which could be better sales copy, discounting, scarcity or whatever.

Your content is the lever. It is the device that will move the load when adequate levels of force are applied. Creating exceptional content is great, but it's just a lever. In engineering terms to gain the mechanical advantage of the lever, you need to have a fulcrum. And the piece that everyone leaves out of the equation is that fulcrum.

The fulcrum is your authority; it's the pivot on which your lever sits to deliver mechanical advantage. Fulcrums deliver more mechanical advantage to the lever requiring less force to lift the load the closer they are to the actual load. That applies nicely to your authority in that the closer you are to your audience (ie the more authority you have) the more mechanical advantage your content has and the less force you need to lift the load.

The next rule we're going to go into is how the Laws of Thermodynamics can help you create better products... Just kidding.

Takeaway Item: Your content is important and it's a great lever to help you make sales, but the key is establishing more authority and using that as the fulcrum to require less force (discounts, scarcity, bonuses, etc.) to convert your audience into customers.

Educate and Indoctrinate Your Audience

Earlier this week I was walking down the street with an Account Manager from the company I work for in my day job. He's a sharp guy, does really well and when he speaks with clients he has the amazing ability some people have to sell without selling.

Needless to say, I was pretty taken aback when he said to me, "Man, you owned that room."

I hadn't really thought about it to be honest, we were with a client for a status update meeting and we were just running through how things were going when the conversation veered towards what comes next. I took that as an opportunity to educate them on what they should do going forward to make the next big step in their business and service delivery.

I told him what I'm about to tell you, "Education is the greatest form of indoctrination that you can employ."

Think about it in a different way.

For the most part, as a society we respect teachers. I'm not just talking about Ms. Davis my Grade 5 teacher, but more broadly this idea includes mentors in business or your kid's hockey coach. People who take the time to share and impart their knowledge on others usually are thought of quite positively.

More importantly, we have an almost inherent trust of teachers... And it goes without saying that trust is a cornerstone of most transactions in business.

I won't bore you with a sermon about the value of the business adage that "customers buy from people they know, like and trust" but it's true and you should remember it.

Teaching delivers all of that to you and more. When you produce content that teaches people something, they immediately gain respect for you.

But here's where maybe what I'm going to share with you veers off from some of the commonly taught ideas of content marketing and into something a bit more practical.

It simply isn't enough to just produce a bunch of "teaching material" put it out as blog posts, podcasts, videos or whatever and expect people to flock to you.

There needs to be more, the "knowing" and "liking" part are incredibly underdone by most people.

If it's appropriate for your market (and it almost always can be), you should try and share more of your personal experiences. I'm not talking about the painful divorce you've just gone through or that you fart and burp more now since having your gallbladder out. Those are probably cases of oversharing.

You can share stories of your experiences with your audience in a tasteful way. We're all hardwired to listen to stories and stories are the best way to teach in my experience. When you tell a story, especially one with a personal element, people begin down the path of not just learning from you, but also getting to know you as a person, not just as someone trying to sell to them.

You've got to be entertaining. I personally use humor (or try to at the very least) to lighten the mood but also get a message across. Other people I know have this knack of telling an incredible story that enthralls you and keeps you wanting more. The key is, interspersing entertainment in your marketing helps people like you and it draws them in towards you.

I want to bring this back full circle to the idea of indoctrination. When used in a sales and marketing context, indoctrination "feels" a bit wrong, but candidly, get over it. You want to teach people things in such a way that they end up getting to know you, they realize that they actually like you and ultimately they trust you enough to do business with them.

It's imperative that as part of the education, you're teaching your prospects and your audience to think the way you want them to think. If you sell managed web hosting, it's not enough to teach people all about the ins and outs of hosting a website, you MUST teach them why managed web hosting is the best option for them and all their friends (remember, always try to generate referrals) and then maybe a bit more subtly why they should choose you.

It goes even deeper than that. The education you're delivering to your clients needs to teach them that what you offer is the best option. I'm not saying beat them over the head with a sales pitch, but presumably you believe what you're selling is great stuff, so make them believe that too. To use our managed web hosting analogy again, if your company is based on Amazon's Cloud, then educate your audience on the value of hyperscale and highly available Cloud services.

This is where it all comes together. Your educational material that you share with clients indoctrinates them on the right way of doing things, which coincidentally is your way of doing things. There needs to be congruence between what you teach and what you sell so that when you position your offer, it becomes a logical decision for them based on what they've been taught by someone they know, like and trust – ie. You.

Before I wrap this rule up, I want to share one mistake I see a lot and am guilty of myself, giving away too much for free. If you sell info products, this is a plague, but even if you sell physical products, you need to be careful about not giving away everything for free. People who make this mistake end up in the business version of the dreaded "friend zone" where you're taken for granted but your needs are never fulfilled, so keep that in mind.

Takeaway Item: Education based marketing is a great way to indoctrinate people not just in what you sell, but it also helps establish authority and build trust. You must take this one step further though and help people get to know you (or your business) and ultimately like you as well as trust you.

Make It Easy For People To Give You Their Money

When I took over the Software-as-a-Service business back in 2006 that I mentioned in the introduction to this book, the first thing that jumped out at me, aside from all of the technical issues, was just how hard it was to actually get customers to give us their money. The business was previously owned by the "eBusiness" unit of a large telco here in Australia and they had all of the accoutrements of a big, slow moving business: arduous contracts, credit management approvals, slow moving account management and of course, meetings... Lots and lots of meetings.

They essentially made it really hard for customers to buy.

This is a plague in some online businesses and it is something you have to be relentless about eliminating in whatever you do.

We've all seen this example:

You get an email telling you about something interesting or maybe you click on an ad on Facebook. You end up on a landing page with a video sales letter.

No price, no "Buy Now" button and the video controls are disabled so you have no ability to see how long you have to wait. Then you have to just sit there and wait… And wait.

I remember back when one guy with a massive list ran a launch and had an 82 minute sales video. You literally didn't see the buy button for 75 minutes. Then he wrote an email to his affiliates for the launch saying the video wasn't converting and he had edited it down to 68 minutes. What a muppet.

Many people will tell you that video sales letters without controls and delayed buy buttons convert better. And maybe they're right. But as a behavior, it sucks. It shows no respect for your prospect's time and more importantly, it shows a lack of confidence in your own product. If you have to force someone to listen to a long winded sales pitch, hide the price and use a bunch of pseudo-persuasion tricks on them, you've got bigger problems.

I personally believe that this costs you sales as well. Some people just want to buy and you should make it easy for them. I call this "Sales Viscosity". You should just make it easy for people to give you their money when they want to.

So how do we do this?

Well, some things are just the technical aspects, but there are also some sales elements that you need to be across.

The technical stuff is pretty easy. You need to have prominent "Buy Now" buttons in logical places on the pages where people can buy things. I don't use any kind of delays or any other tricks, just simple buttons.

Another technical problem that you need to be across is cart abandonment. There's an element to sales psychology with the whole shopping cart process, but that's not relevant to this rule. This rule relates to "Sales Viscosity" and having a process with a lot of steps or requiring too much information will hurt your sales. One reason PayPal works so well is it's easy for people.

I am guilty of having broken this rule myself a few times particularly around the convoluted checkout process. When we first started offering our customers our RapidAction Writing services, we had a whole checkout process using the WooCommerce shopping cart. My logic was that having a cart would allow people to pick and choose multiple writing products and then checkout.

Except nobody ever did this. They usually wanted one thing, but I made them go through four or five pages. It was stupid and didn't make sense.

When we switched to simple landing pages with built in order forms, conversions went way up. We effectively lubricated the sales process and made it easier for our customers to fill in a single form and give us their money.

Seems all very simple in hindsight.

Takeaway Item: Don't be a sales inhibitor in your online business. Complexity, trickery and opaqueness make it very hard for people to buy stuff for a variety of reasons. The best thing you can do is to make it as easy as possible for people to give you their money.

You're In The Traffic Business

Interesting side note to this rule before I begin. I wrote this rule in a Facebook post back in June 2015 about six months before I started on this book. To be honest, this is the rule that started this whole process. After posting it to Facebook, I wrote it in a new note in Evernote. Then I started writing down the occasional idiom that I thought of periodically. To me though, this is one of the foundational rules of running an online business successfully.

Right now, if you're just starting to learn about how to market your business online or do any kind of internet marketing, I'd almost certainly guess that you are being subjected to the absolute greatest con job I've seen in my nearly ten years' experience.

There is a whole industry that's sprung up around the idea of not worrying about getting traffic, just focus on producing good content and traffic will take care of itself. That's a lie. I can't state that plainly enough.

Essentially what you are being told is that the internet fairies will ride in on their magical unicorns bringing hordes of starving buyers with them as long as you "create epic content." Elsewhere in this book there's a whole rule around building "corn fields, not baseball fields" so I won't get into that right now beyond just pointing it out.

What I do want you to learn is that online, first and foremost, you are in the traffic business. I'm not talking about getting gobs of cheap and meaningless traffic either, anyone can do that.

Let me start by giving you an example of generating traffic incorrectly.

There used to be a person who sold an info product on Udemy about using Facebook Ads to build traffic. That's a valuable topic in and of itself except in this course what the guy was teaching was to go get $0.01 "Likes" from third world countries to your Facebook page to show "social proof". Watching this course it's like the idiot circus has come to town and I've got a front row seat under the big top. This is a classic example of bad traffic. You don't want bad traffic, especially if you're paying for it, that's lunacy.

Being in the traffic business is about driving leads that are most likely to convert into customers to your home base and your offers. You are not just trying to attract the right people to you, you're actively trying to dissuade the wrong people from coming to your site at all.

Attracting the right sort of people to you is obvious, but the dissuading the wrong people often is perplexing for people new to any form of traffic generation. The idea is pretty simple. I think of traffic generation as me trying to gain the attention of someone. I inherently place a value on other people's attention and time. If I'm using crappy clickbait titles or trying to trick them into giving me their attention, I'm wasting their time. That's not cool.

Conversely, when you have something of value to offer someone and you make them aware of it, it's a good experience for everyone. You're helping that person, they gain respect for you and ideally, they start doing business with you.

Which leads us nicely to the idea that there are two parts to your online efforts at the most basic level: your offers and traffic. These two things are inextricably linked. Generating traffic and having nothing to offer is a waste of time just like having an offer with no traffic is a pointless exercise.

I'm going to assume that you have an offer.

One simple secret to success is making sure that the traffic you are generating should be congruent with your offer. I use the word "congruence" a fair bit because it is a critical part of successful marketing, but with traffic it is especially important.

Let's imagine you sell lawn mowers. Now we're going to focus your offer on an even more specific market, high priced, ride-on lawn mowers to people in Wichita, Kansas. Ranking #1 in Google across the entire world for "ride-on mowers" would be great and it would probably generate a substantial amount of traffic, but most people probably won't buy. The money you're paying and the effort you are expending to achieve that outcome really isn't getting a great return.

The same effort could be spent figuring out how to target the most affluent suburbs in Wichita with high levels of owner occupiers. If you could spend $10 targeting that specific group, versus $10 targeting everyone in the whole world interested in high end ride-on mowers, it's obvious which would get a better result for your business.

Measuring your traffic results is a vital piece of this. You need to make sure that you are properly tracking the right traffic metrics. Knowing what traffic sources are generating leads and which sources convert best into sales and profit is the place you want to be in. I see people all the time talking about how their visitor numbers grow because they wrote an epic blog post, but their customer numbers are flat. That's a sign your traffic business is not on track. You mustn't confuse quantity with quality!

Here's an interesting way to think about measuring and analyzing your traffic for business benefit. Your accountant is able to produce a multitude of spreadsheets that show you how your business is doing: profit, cash flow, liabilities, revenue growth month on month, etc... You should be thinking of your traffic the same way. I also thought it would be cool to effectively have a "traffic accountant" in your business. For most of us, that's probably an overhead we can't afford, but having a small change in positioning when we think about traffic can result in a pretty big positive mindset shift.

Takeaway Item: Traffic is the lifeblood of any business on the internet. No traffic, no business. It really is that simple. You need to make sure you're focusing your traffic efforts on targeting the right people and measuring the right things to get a maximum return on your effort.

Plant Corn, Not Baseball Fields

In the rule "You're in the Traffic Business" I highlighted the "content marketing lie" that is being perpetuated by many people who teach online marketing. Just to recap, people are being told to stop worrying about actively going out and generating traffic, just create "epic content" and the gods of the interwebz will intervene and deliver to you an admiring audience, wallets in hand and flush with cash they are desperate to give you.

The lie is convenient and it is predicated on laziness.

Think about it, it's pretty easy to write a blog post. In this single writing session, I've written over 2000 words for this book. It wasn't hard. Replace blog post with podcast or a video for YouTube and it adds a layer of technical complexity but again, in and of itself it isn't hard.

But imagine if we took that video you created, posted it on a Wordpress site we set up for you and asked you to generate

113

traffic for it, that's hard. Creating good, even great content is fundamentally easier than promoting it and generating consistent high quality traffic to it.

Which leads me to the title of this rule, "Plant Corn, Not Baseball Fields."

That's obviously a play on the premise of the classic Kevin Costner movie, "Field of Dreams". If you're one of the nine people on the planet who hasn't seen the movie, basically Costner's character has blind faith that the voices he's hearing telling him to rip out his corn fields and create a baseball diamond will save his farm. Costner builds the baseball field, wanders around the country chasing ghosts, risks financial ruin but in the end through the magic of Hollywood everything works out.

It's a great movie. But it's a movie. The better business strategy for Costner's character would have been to replant the corn and figure out how to improve his harvesting capability or diversify his crops. That said, I doubt anyone would pay to go see that movie.

Having any kind of entrepreneurial spirit requires you to be an optimist at some level, but you have to have more than hope. Hope is not a plan.

Most people teaching content marketing are effectively telling you to bank on serendipity. That's just foolish and over the past few years, it is the #1 cause of frustration, disappointment and wasted time that I've seen from people trying to break into building an online business.

These people are building baseball diamonds instead of planting corn.

You need to think about your efforts strategically. You want to build assets that will accrue in value over time and help deliver exponentially more profit. You're looking to create momentum in your business.

The best assets you can build in your online business are your market authority, strongly converting offers and an email list of engaged buyers and leads. Everything you do needs to be focused on maximizing the value of those assets and utilizing them to generate income. And it's not enough to do just one of those things, you need to be doing them all concurrently.

Creating great content is a massive part of that, but on its own, it's kind of worthless. You need to be out promoting that content, sharing it with people who can most benefit from it and making them aware that you are someone who can help them.

And that content has to work hard, it needs to have a job. It's not enough just to write an informative piece or create a great video, your content has to build your authority, make an offer or get people to optin to your email list. Sometimes it can do all three. That's the marketing part of content marketing!

I used the word momentum earlier and that's a critical aspect of your success. When you're starting out, you're just not going to have any momentum so everything will seem like hard work. Once you start building your assets, then it becomes considerably easier to get things done.

Takeaway Item: Good businesses focus on building assets that they can leverage to gain momentum and generate revenue over the long term. Everything you do should be focused on building and contributing to the success of your core assets in your online business.

Pricing Is Hard And You Will Get It Wrong

I'm putting it out there right now, just like the title of this rule says, pricing is hard and you will get it wrong. Give yourself a free pass and stop worrying over it.

As I mentioned before, when we started RapidAction Writing we built up a fairly significant white label client base because we provided great quality content, reasonably quickly at a stupidly low price. In fact, it was too low. Our white label customers basically consumed all of our supply and nearly suffocated our ability to deliver.

At first we were pretty happy because it's very scary to launch a new business venture and the high volumes validated our service offering. Quickly though it became obvious that we'd priced ourselves too low. Our profit margins were too small, so to scale our capacity to deliver meant that we were taking on additional risk.

It was an honest mistake, but like a lot of mistakes that online business owners make, we tried to work around it rather than deal with it swiftly. On our site where we were trying to generate more organic sales from colder traffic, we started inching up the prices and offering higher value services at increased prices.

The thing was, our pricing problem was with our white label clients not people who hadn't bought anything from us yet. The demand coming from our site from organic traffic was pretty light, so whether we were charging $18 or $30 per 500 words didn't really matter, it was the guys buying 40 and 50 articles at a time for $14 per 500 words and needing them within 10 days that were the problem.

Finally, I just came to the conclusion that I needed to sort it out once and for all. We hiked our prices on our site for our commercial customers and gave our white label customers 30 days notice that our prices were increasing to the publicly listed prices but bulk discounts could be negotiated.

What happened next might not surprise you... We lost a lot of business. Going from $14 - 18 per 500 words up to $50 per 500 words just meant that for some of our white label clients our content was too expensive for them to make a profit on. A few complained, but the reality was we'd ended up with this white label business by happenstance rather than design, so while I empathized, the reality was our margins weren't good enough.

The other thing that happened will probably surprise you considering that I said we lost a lot of business... We started making more money. More revenue, more profit.

What actually happened was probably a bit of luck and just a confluence of external events occurring at the right time. We'd been doing it long enough that we'd built up a significant lead flow and the price rise coincided with the timing of their buying decision so in essence, newly acquired clients paying more made up for the lost clients who were paying less.

But another funny thing happened, the choir of bad advice from internet marketers started singing. Numerous people started saying that everyone should charge more and that "if in doubt, double your price." Our good fortune started being heralded as validation of stupid ideas by the idiot fringe.

I personally think in retrospect we made the right move on pricing at the time. We started low and increased our prices over time to reflect what the market would bear and we recognized the limits of our supply chain. That's basic Keynesian economics - demand outstripped supply and the price increased to balance them out.

I recently told a copywriter online who asked me for advice about pricing, "Think of an amount that if a client offered it to you, you'd rip their hand off shaking it to accept the deal. Then think about a dollar amount that if they offered you that fee you'd decline because it wasn't worth your time. The price you should charge is in the middle of those two figures."

I don't want to be one of those goofballs who make meme posts and quote themselves on Facebook, but I do think that's a pretty good way to think about pricing services work where you're actually performing the service. If you are outsourcing or you have input costs, for example if you're selling a physical product, then you need to weigh up those expenses and costs to factor those into your price.

One thing to remember is that when you're starting out, almost everyone has a propensity to doubt themselves and therefore you undervalue what you're worth. We all do it. The one suggestion I would have when you're just starting out and you're not sure about your pricing, is to try and avoid locking yourself into too many longer term deals at your initial price point. While it may seem really attractive to bank that revenue, you may also be massively undervaluing yourself and it will be much harder to change.

The overall principle still stands though. Figure out a price that you think is fair, you'd be happy to receive from clients and go from there. Don't over think it too much and certainly try not to stress about it.

Takeaway Item: Establishing your prices can be challenging and stressful. It's important to remember not to let this hold you back from selling. Put your stake in the ground and be prepared to change as you get more comfortable with what your customers will pay.

Beware Vanity Metrics

Whenever you spend any time on the internet and paying attention to people who are doing online marketing, you start to notice a whole bunch of strange numbers being monitored and reported on. You see dashboards that track "Likes" and "Retweets", elegant graphs showing how many people visit a site and often a dizzying array of other numbers.

And none of them actually mean anything. They're vanity metrics. They look good on a chart or graph and they give the site owner a sense of achievement, but the truth is, they are generally quite worthless.

You can't pay your rent in Likes or Retweets. You don't walk into a Mercedes dealership, pick out the car you want, then fire up your laptop and say to the sales guy, "Blammy! 18,000 uniques baby! When do I pick up my car?"

The world doesn't work like that.

Now, most people know this, but there's something that goes tragically wrong when people get online for awhile, they seem to lose sight of these basic concepts. Their ideas of success morph into this intangible nothingness.

So I'm going to set you straight with this rule, the one single number above all else that you should be interested in is net profit. The money at the end of the month that is left over after you pay all of your bills and taxes, the money you get to keep.

Everything else is just a sideshow.

Before you spin out and start sending me hate mail, let me just say that there are other numbers worth tracking as well, especially the ones that act as an early warning indicator of future profit or problems on the horizon. They're important management metrics absolutely, but the main score that matters is net profit.

I don't feel the need to teach you what net profit is, you should already know that and if you don't, then you shouldn't even be considering doing business online or anywhere else for that matter. But what I do want to talk a little bit about are some of those ancillary numbers that can give you an idea of where you're headed.

Earlier in this rule, I dismissed unique visitors as something of a vanity metric and I stand by that. If you want to sell something online, then it goes without saying that you need visitors, but knowing how many people come to your site in isolation is more or less worthless data, you can't really take any action on it. What you really want to be tracking are the sources of your traffic. Where are people coming from to get to your site.

The big one is obviously organic traffic which largely comes from Google. You may also be getting traffic from Facebook, Twitter and the other social platforms more broadly. There may be people coming from particular websites or forums as well. A strong site has a variety of traffic sources.

Knowing where people come from is important because it allows you to target your marketing efforts more closely. Then when you do a month over month comparison to see your traffic growth or decline on a source basis, you can see the impact of your efforts.

There are a bunch of indicator metrics that you can have for leads. In simple terms a lead is someone that's show an interest in what you have to offer and predominantly, these people join your email list. Most people will tell you that having a "big" list is better, but that's not necessarily true.

I'm pretty simple, I really only care about revenue per lead in aggregate over time. How much money do my emails make over the course of say a year, per lead? This lets me know what the average lead is worth to me, that way I know what I can afford to spend to acquire a lead. If each person on my list is worth $50/yr in revenue, then I know that I can spend $10 to acquire a lead and it should be profitable within the first quarter.

Quick call out, one thing I don't pay any attention to with email are open rates and even click rates. I'm interested in tracking how much money I make per email. Open rates in particular is one of the worst vanity metrics that people track.

Conversion rates are another good thing to track, but don't go overboard. Knowing how well your sales pages convert into sales is pretty important because improving that number is free money. Think about it, if you have 1000 people hit your sales page per month and 1% buy a $100 product, you're making $1000. If you can improve that page's conversion rate to 1.5%, then you make an additional $500 on the same volume of traffic.

Like I said, don't go overboard. I've seen people get lost in the minutiae of conversion optimization and get really excited about miniscule results. Stick to the big things like sales page conversions and increasing your optin conversion rate. Those two numbers track how effectively you're turning people into leads and sales and those are obviously very good numbers to know.

Depending on the type of business you're in, there could be a variety of other leading indicators you may want to know about or metrics you want to track. For instance, if you have a recurring product or service, lowering your churn rate is probably one of the most important things in your entire business. Someone who podcasts may want to track downloads because that's what advertisers are interested in despite it being a worthless number. Horses for courses.

At the end of the day, knowing your numbers is vital, but the only one that REALLY matters is your net profit number.

Takeaway Item: Avoid tracking numbers that look good to people on the internet, but aren't really indicative of how your business is going. Net profit is the bottom line score for how successful you are and you need to find the leading indicator numbers for your business that will help you manage performance.

Pay Peanuts, Get Monkeys

I just believe at a fundamental level that something is worth, more or less, what you're willing to pay for it. Immediately people will start thinking "price = money" but that's not always the case. Your time is worth something. Your attention is worth something. When you do anything, you're paying a price in time and attention and those are resources that could be spent on something else.

Let me give you a classic example in the online marketing world, logo and graphics creation.

You see people all the time go on Fiverr or Upwork and look to pay $25 for a new design for their website. Now, that's not to say that you won't get a great design for $25, but chances are you'll probably get something that isn't what I would consider top shelf.

There are two things at play here: one, they are underestimating the effort of getting something high quality and the skill required; and two, they are being cheap because they don't really value the design.

In an office environment, this kind of thing happens all the time. You sit in a meeting, an idea somehow manages to achieve escape velocity from the gravitational well of stupidity that most internal meetings generate and then it comes time to figure out how to actually execute this idea. Without doubt, the responsibility will be given to someone who already has a full plate and probably wasn't in the room. That just says that the idea isn't respected enough to assign adequate resources necessary to achieve the desired outcome.

In your online business, if something is worth doing, it is worth properly paying for it to be done well. That constitutes a couple of elements:

- If you are going to outsource the work, hire the best person you can afford to complete the task as quickly as possible at a high level of quality;
- Assign some time to properly set expectations, review and manage the outsourcer; and,
- Show appreciation and gratitude for the person completing the work.

The first two are just time and money things that speak to my earlier points, if something is worth doing then you need to pay the right price. I run the money aspect through a simple mental exercise of, "If this thing I want costs more than X, then I'd rather do it myself or not have it at all." Take a logo as an example, some people pay thousands of dollars, for me, I'd rather do something simple myself in an hour or two if the price is over $500.

Pretty simple, but effective logic.

The last point around showing appreciation is a tricky one that most people don't do enough of. I believe that gratitude and appreciation are like currency. You assign a value to them, other people assign their own value to them and you can exchange them. When you're working with someone, even if you are paying them to do the work, a simple "Thanks for your effort, you're doing a good job" will go pretty far.

The worst experiences I've ever had in my online business almost always come from when I run across a client that has been cheap or looked for the lowest cost option for important work. In our SEO business over the years we've come across sites which have tanked because the third world SEO company they are using have built hundreds of dodgy links. When you point this out to the client, they often say, "But I paid good money! I spent $200 with them for this. We get most of our traffic from organic and now our business is in jeopardy!"

I never have this problem because from an early age it was instilled into me that you get what you pay for. We didn't really have much money and I played ice hockey which is a very expensive sport. When I got to high school, I would often pocket my lunch money to save up enough to buy a $35 stick that was better and lasted longer than a $20 stick that wasn't as good.

The last point I'd probably make is around simplification and simply not doing things. Sometimes we get ideas and decide we want something done, so we look for a cheap and quick option. Whenever I start thinking like this I pause and ask, "Do I really need this?" Often you'll find that you don't need that thing at all and by just not getting it you actually simplify your business and make it easier to run.

Takeaway Item: You get what you pay for. If you don't have a lot of money or you don't think something is worth spending up on, then you're going to get average or worse results. Sometimes it is better to do nothing - think about whether you "need" something of it you just "want" it.

Section 5

Rules You Should Know and Never Forget

Put Down Your Technology Toys

I've probably said it a hundred times in this book, but I'll say it again... I'm a pretty technical guy. As a result, all of the latest toys and gadgets interest me. I get excited to try them out to find what their limits are and how I can bend them to my will.

It can become a bit problematic though. A few years back we were revamping one of our websites and for some reason, I'd remembered a blog post I'd read a week earlier talking about how fast Google's Cloud Compute Engine was. For some reason I thought it would be a great idea to spin up an instance and test it. Then I realized that getting Wordpress working on it was a challenge. Two days later I had Wordpress running on the Compute Engine and it was faster... The speed difference was imperceptible it was so small, but I'd done it. Meanwhile, the website we were meant to relaunch took an extra week.

I could rattle off a thousand stories like that one from my past experiences. Luckily over the last year or so, I've made a conscious effort to not do that to myself anymore. And boy oh boy has it become apparent how many other people are getting utterly lost in the technology these days.

There isn't a day that goes by where I don't see at least a dozen people writing on one Facebook group or another about the struggles they are having trying to get their landing page creator to work with their shopping cart system or some idiosyncratic plugin is causing a conflict that's causing their backups to fail. It is like watching a slow motion train wreck with some people - I know it's going to end in tears, but there's nothing you can do to convince them to take a step back.

This affliction affects two different classes of people: one, the propeller heads like myself who are really into the technology; and two, the do-it-yourselfers who aren't terribly technical but may know enough to make themselves dangerous.

The impact for each of those two groups manifests itself in different ways. For the propeller heads, they see something that can be done better with technology, head off to the batcave and beaver away. They get the solution to 95% complete with relative ease. For most people, this would be way more functionality than they could ever hope to want or use, but for this group, that other 5% will happen! With me personally, that's when the swearing starts and it's 50/50 that I will ever get the flux capacitors into alignment, but plenty of time gets wasted.

For the DIY'ers it's an entirely different story. They watch the sales videos for the technology, they immediately misunderstand what it can do, so they buy it without hesitation. The next day they get stuck into making this new optin plugin they bought process credit card transactions because "surely it can do that too." Nine emails to support later and six Facebook posts to various groups asking the same question and they can't figure out why they are so lost. Why can't this stuff just be easy like in the video?!?

I'm going to share with you one of the greatest secrets that I've learned in all my years of online business and from nearly twenty years of working in Enterprise IT... Simplicity. Yep, just try and use as little technology as humanly possible to get your desired outcome and not another bit more. The moment you start trying to "tweak" or enhance stuff, you're screwed. You're heading down a path that will end in tears.

For people just getting started in their online business, I recommend that they use as little technology as possible. A simple Wordpress site hosted with a solid company like LiquidWeb, a means of taking money like PayPal and an email service provider like ActiveCampaign or Aweber. That's pretty much everything you need to get started. It might look a bit janky at first and it won't be the all singing, all dancing experience that some people offer, but it will work!

It might seem odd that someone as technical as I am is espousing an approach that tells you to minimize your use of technology tools, especially in an online business. The truth is, there are two massive time wasters that I see too many people get trapped in: one, is the guru merry-go-round of crazy; and two, trying to implement insane levels of marketing technology into their business.

You don't need the latest funnel generator with add on automated webinar software when you are just getting started. Focus on finding your audience, attracting them to you and building/creating great products and services that will make them happy. That should be your primary goal, not having an adaptive feature box that integrates with your email drip system.

Put the tech toys away. You'll thank me for it someday.

Takeaway Item: With great technology comes great time wasting. Make sure you maintain a "simple is best" approach and delay integrating more technology until you absolutely must.

Consume What You Buy, Don't Be A Collector

One of the dirty secrets that everyone selling digital products online knows is that the majority of people who buy your info product, video training course, Wordpress plugin or SaaS app will never use it. Numbers vary, but I can tell you from first-hand experience, that about 75% of the people who bought my various Udemy courses over the past year have never looked at a single lecture. I also know that I have customers who routinely buy content from our writing business and never publish it online.

These people are often referred to as "collectors". They buy products and services all the time online but never actually use them for anything. For some people, they convince themselves that eventually they'll find a use for the latest "InstaPinBook+" plugin or that getting access to that lead page builder at the launch price of $99/mth is a good investment for the future when they'll need to start churning out landing pages.

There's another group who just get a rush from buying something that looks cool. I've heard it said that these people are happy to buy because, "they get their dopamine drip".

All collectors are really suffering from "Shiny Object Syndrome". They see something new, they want it and they start rationalizing the purchase. A product or service with really good marketing often exacerbates this but the reality is these people were probably going to buy no matter what.

Being a collector has a couple of downsides. The obvious one is the cost. It is very easy to sign up to some monthly recurring products and services, but much more difficult to get out of them. There is a percentage of every recurring program where the customers don't even remember they are subscribed and just get charged to their PayPal or Credit Card every month. Also, if you end up in a few recurring programs, it doesn't take long before you're racking up $200 - $300 per month in small recurring charges. I've seen people paying for Infusionsoft and Ontraport for months at US$300+ each and not using either.

The other downside is that when you do want to solve a problem, the collector often has so many tools at their disposal they end up confusing themselves to the point of inactivity. I spoke to a lady recently who asked for help setting up the front end of her funnel and our first conversation began with, "I have LeadPages, ClickFunnels and ThriveThemes, I can't work out which to use!"

If it ended there you'd think she was just lured in once, but it carried on. She had ActiveCampaign, MailChimp and Aweber accounts for email despite having a list of less than 200 people. She also had SamCart, GravityForms, PayPal, Stripe and an assortment of other products and services.

She was just entirely overwhelming herself by buying things. When we actually got into constructing her offer and her funnel she had a very clear idea of what she wanted. In fact, her value proposition and offer were really strong, but for months she'd dithered doing nothing because she couldn't work out how to piece it all together with the dozens of products she'd bought.

What I recommend for everyone I come in contact with is that unless you have an immediate need for something, don't buy it. That goes for software products, Kindle books, Udemy courses and everything else you can buy online. Make sure that everything you buy gets used and before you buy something else, look to see if you can reuse something you already have!

Takeaway Item: Buying too many services and products wastes money and ends up confusing you on what you should use. Only buy what you need immediately.

Minimum Viable Product Is Not Code For Garbage

Back when I was running the SaaS business, we adopted the Agile Development process for managing our team and deliverables. We also used a bit of SCRUM, had functional sprinting, tracked our "tech debt" and we were really focused in getting software into the hands of users to test.

It worked like a charm. We turned out a massive piece of software that had taken our competitors years to build in just under 15 months. Most importantly, the software was better and more functional.

We shipped a minimum viable product before that term had really entered the general lexicon. Basically, there were some advanced features that people wanted and we knew we could deliver, but we really needed to ship the product and get people using it so that we maintained focus on delivering the best quality product.

When I heard the term minimum viable product for the first time a few years after that I totally understood what the person was talking about. It's an approach to developing complex software that makes a ton of sense, especially for smaller teams in difficult or competitive markets.

Then marketers got ahold of the term. Worse than that, internet marketers started using it. Like most things that internet marketers latch onto it, they basically infused it with ample doses of scam and laziness.

When I see someone talking about their MVP for their info product or some such nonsense, something inside of me dies a little. They've turned the MVP concept into a big "make money online" scam where they deliver a half assed unfinished product and if enough people buy it, they do enough just to finish it with as little effort as possible... Maybe. I've seen more than my fair share of "MVP" products never get finished or fixed as the creator moves on to something else more interesting.

For a second, put aside the fact that I think selling half finished products is a stupid idea, but just focus on what people call them, "Minimum Viable Product". Where the idea of an MVP is being abused is that focus for some people is on the wrong part of the term.

When I think of MVP, I think the most important part is "viable". The product has to fulfill its core purpose, that's what viable means! It may not have all the bells and whistles or nice to have elements you'll eventually deliver, but the person using it is going to say, "This is great! It does exactly what I need it to do and it will be above and beyond when it's done." You're delivering a viable product in its minimal form.

Unfortunately, what I now see is, people focusing on the "minimum" part primarily. It's almost like they ask themselves, "What is the minimum amount of work I can do to create something that would be financially viable for me to make." It's a subtle play on words but when you look at it holistically what's happening in this instance is the product creator is looking at it purely from their selfish perspective. What's the least work they can do and still make some money. I think you can make the MVP model of product creation work for you in your online business. In fact, I'm doing it with my Casual Marketer business.

Let me walk you through it:

The core offering is the monthly physically newsletter, so I need to get that planned and ready to be delivered. In and of itself, creating the monthly newsletter, printing it up and having it delivered to subscribers is the minimum viable product. This is what customers are buying, that's the offer. From Day One, if you subscribe, you should feel that you get what you pay for.

Then there's this book. I decided about a month before the launch to create this book and give it away to subscribers of my Casual Marketer Monthly Newsletter, at least initially. I launched the newsletter without the book and people still were getting what they paid for. Then when the book was done, I sent it to all existing subscribers retrospectively and when someone new subscribes, they get it sent to them right away.

I've also thought about making my info products and training programs freely available to all of my subscribers. I'm not sure how I want to do that and I may have to re-record some of it. While I'd like to offer that, I made the call that it's not fundamental to the Newsletter product, so it is not part of my "minimum viable product" for Casual Marketer. As a result, it will maybe come later on depending on the take up and feedback.

The point of explaining this to you is to demonstrate that the concept of MVP can work for just about any business. It works really well in the software industry, but it can work for info products and other types of online businesses. It's all about understanding your offer, putting your customer's best interests at the center of your thinking and committing yourself to delivering high quality outcomes.

Takeaway Item: Creating a Minimum Viable Product is a great way to deliver outcomes to your customers and yourself in a highly iterative fashion. The key is to not think about doing the minimal amount of work, but to consider what a minimum, cut down version of your product that delivers all the core outcomes for your customer would actually look like.

Master The Pareto Principle

This rule goes together very nicely with the "Minimum Viable Product Is Not Code For Garbage" and "Do One Thing At A Time" rules. They really could be thought of as a triumvirate of rules around delivering good outcomes for customers in the most efficient and effective way possible.

For those of your not aware, the Pareto Principle is more commonly known as the "80/20 rule." Vilfredo Pareto was an early 20th century Italian economist who observed that 20% of the people owned 80% of the wealth. Others have taken the Pareto Principle and made observations of how this principle applies in a variety of other parts of life such as 80% of bugs in software come from just 20% of the code or that 20% of your staff provide 80% of your value.

I am an ardent believer in this rule and therefore, I will try and indoctrinate you into believing it as well. That's my job.

Let's start with a few observations that I'd like to take credit for, but I'm sure other people have found the same thing.

I notice in our online services businesses that 80% of all of the revenue (and profit) come from just 20% of the clients. These are the regular clients who really get the value in what we do and they keep coming back or are on recurring payment programs. In any business, these are your best customers, you need to identify them and you need to make sure they're happy. The bonus element of this is that the top performing 20% of customers also generate 80% of our referrals.

The 80/20 rule is not always positive though, I can also point to 20% of our customers that create 80% of support requests. This is important for us because it demonstrates a few things that need to be looked at more closely. In some instances, there's something not working effectively with our onboarding process which is causing friction for some of our customers. In all likelihood though, there's a significant portion of that 20% of customers who aren't a good fit for us and their business is often unprofitable, so we need to fix these cases or cease doing business with these particular customers.

The last example I will use is around leads. About 80% of our best leads come from around 20% of our lead sources. There are forums or Facebook groups that consistently generate most of our leads. By knowing that, I can spend more time in those places, lifting my profile because I know it's a good use of my time. I can also start looking for other places online that have similar demographics, so I can start testing those to see if they work for lead generation.

There is one more interesting thing that I've seen some people do with customers and the 80/20 rule and that's take it down to a second level. If 20% of your customers generate 80% of your profit, what would happen if you took that down another level. What you end up with is 4% of customers generating 64% of profit. Now you can hyper-target that 4% and make sure they are really satisfied.

Obviously, these observations may not apply directly to your business, but I'd be willing to bet that you have your own 80/20 instances. These might be positive or negative in nature, which underlines the importance of doing the work to understand them. If you can find 20% of something in your business that's generating 80% of your costs, you then know where you can best focus to find savings and efficiencies.

The last thing I'd suggest is that you be disciplined about reviewing your business to find these situations. Everyone spends a great deal of time working on their profit & loss spreadsheet or putting together a dashboard about how many tickets were raised this month, but not enough people dive into the detail behind these numbers to find the patterns and understand what's causing them.

And that's really the advantage of looking for the Pareto Principle across the various aspects of your business. You're probably really busy, just like me and the time we have to work on things is limited, so trying to understand why things are happening or spending our time on things that deliver the most additional value is critical to your success.

Takeaway Item: The Pareto Principle (the 80/20 rule) seems to crop up over and over again in business. Identify these trends in your business and find ways to maximize your overall value by spending time optimizing the patterns you uncover.

Perfect Is The Enemy Of Good Enough

I'm going to let you in on a little secret… I like to tinker with stuff. I am a pretty technical individual and when something isn't exactly how I want it to be, I'm quite content to sit there and work on it until it is.

That is a colossal waste of time and it drives my wife nuts when it comes to our online business activities. I'm not OCD or anything quite like that, I just want stuff to behave the way I want it to work. I have an inner drive to bend technology to my will.

At some point in late 2015, I decided that I'm going to just focus on getting things done and getting them out there. It's a big challenge for someone like me.

And that's an aphorism that you should become familiar with, "Perfect is the Enemy of Good Enough." Some people have morphed that into "Perfect is the Enemy of Done" and I'm ok with that one too.

The problem for most people is that when they put something online that they are heavily involved with, it becomes an extension of themselves. All kinds of insecurities kick in at this point and you start dissecting everything to the Nth degree.

Stop doing that. Stop it right now. It will never be perfect. Your lizard brain won't let it.

Let it go.

Whew... I don't know about you, but I feel better having just written that.

What you eventually come to realize is that most people look past the superficialities if what you're producing has the value that they're looking for. This is where you need to spend your time making sure the content itself is top shelf, that it's the best that you can deliver and not just a meaningless discussion on what shade of blue the drop down hover effect of your nav icons are for a site that nobody visits.

Am I saying that your stuff should be horrific and ugly? No, that would be stupid. Professionalism is important and a certain level of aesthetic pleasantness is instinctively attributed to professionalism. But it doesn't need to be pixel perfect.

The other caveat I'd put out there is that if you're in a highly aesthetic market or something very visual then that's part of your offering so it needs to be on point. I had a short term coaching client one time that made designer cupcakes. She wanted some help getting her business a higher profile online and the first comment I made was, "Are those your best photos? You should get them professionally shot." Then I pointed out that her website looked like it was made by a five-year-old with crayons who'd lost their thumbs and vision in a horrible boating accident.

I said short-term coaching client because we parted ways after that session. She wanted to talk about funnels and email marketing, but I kept pointing out that her stuff looked subpar for her target audience. Nobody wants to buy ugly cupcakes for their husband's fiftieth birthday party.

So how do we get past this desire to tinker and make things "just right"?

For me the trick is keeping multiple notes running in Evernote. One note is all of the high level features or things I have to do on a project. Then for each of those features I create a note of its own. While I'm working on a feature, if I run across something that isn't quite right or needs more work, I just make a quick note in that feature's Evernote note and I move on.

This approach lets me focus on getting the big stuff out of the way, finishing my projects and then swing back around and clean up the stuff I'm not happy with later.

I can't trick you into finishing your work and frankly, we're all adults so I can't even be bothered making the effort. I'm just trying to make you aware of the problem and give you a different perspective. Deep down, if you have this problem you probably think you'll feel bad about the stuff that isn't perfect, but I promise, you'll feel better about finishing something and it will overwhelm that nagging sense of imperfection.

Takeaway Item: Voltaire was a smart French guy. He quoted an Italian guy named Pascetti, so Pascetti must have been really smart. They basically said that, "best or better is the enemy of good". I tend to listen to smart French philosophers quoting even smarter Italians. You should too. Just focus on getting things done, put them out there and clean them up later, you'll feel so much better about yourself and you'll make way more progress!

Model Success, Don't Rip It Off

I touched on people completely copying stuff to the point of it being totally ineffective in the rule "Don't Get Caught Buying Hope", but really this topic deserves its own rule.

There are so many people out on the internet doing genuinely innovative marketing that you'd be crazy not to look at what they are doing and trying to figure out how you can apply it to your situation.

But that doesn't mean blatantly copy it.

There are two reasons for this:

You look like a clown when you effectively steal someone's marketing and apply it to your own online business; and,
It won't work for you because it hasn't been designed for your business.

Let me give you an example to show you what I mean.

My mate Dan Norris started a business called WPCurve. They do lightweight Wordpress support tasks for a fixed monthly fee. It's an interesting productized service model and Dan marketed it very well.

As soon as people realized Dan was having some success the copycats arrived. Some were just copying his model and maybe making it cheaper by a few bucks per month - pretty lame stuff, but really rather benign. There was one other "company" that literally ripped off his entire website and weren't even smart enough to change some of the URL names.

The rip-offs looked like complete clowns. They will never get any real traction because the broader community know they are copycats at best. That's a very limited business.

The other thing is, they really couldn't compete with Dan because they were forever chasing him. They were hoping to get in his slipstream and let him pull them along, but they just didn't have the mental horsepower to pass him. They were looking at what he's doing now and trying to keep up, he was looking at what he was doing next and racing forward.

So how could you look at something like what Dan had done successfully and apply that to your business? That's the real skill that you need to develop. How can you model success rather than just rip it off blindly?

Modelling success is actually easier than you think, but it requires that you look at things perhaps a little differently than you're used to. When I see something that is successful I try and look past the superficial things that are "done well" and look for the underlying thing that is driving success.

For example, you might see a company that does customer onboarding well, has top notch support, easy to use site navigation and great email communication. These are all individual pieces that are tactically well done, but when you dig deeper you realize that the focus is on delivering an exceptional customer experience. That focus permeates everything and so the individual touch points with the customer are all highly optimized.

That's what I mean about digging past the superficialities and looking at the underlying driver. You aren't trying to replicate the "what" you're trying to understand the "why".

Once I get to the "why" I then look at how I can apply that same lens on whatever I'm doing. I'm not going to copy their process for onboarding customers, but I'm going to take away and figure out how to apply it in a way that makes sense for me, my business and my customers.

Since writing and publishing the Members Edition of this book, Dan and his partner Alex have sold WPCurve to internet services juggernaut, GoDaddy. This further makes my point because the copycats will never have that kind of success, they're just playing the wrong game and doing so from behind.

Takeaway Item: Copying is a strategy for losers. When you see something successful, get past the superficial signs and figure out the motivating driver of the successful activity. Once you understand why something successful works the way it does, you can then work on applying those learnings to your own business.

Fire Crappy Customers

One of the best pieces of advice I've ever received came from a boss I used to have about ten years ago. The SaaS company I was running was primarily focused on the construction industry and for those of you who've had anything to do with that particular industry, you'll know first-hand that they have a considerably higher percentage of horrible people to deal with.

This one very small contractor started using our system just as we were deploying our newest version. My business development team warned them that this was pretty new software and their experience may be mixed initially. We were also quite concerned that they kept describing the project they were putting on our system as having a high profile within a difficult client.

Despite my staff doing everything we could to convince them to use our older, more stable (but less attractive and less functional) version, they insisted that they were paying for the latest and greatest and that's what they wanted.

Almost right away the problems started. They were a smaller company and didn't have the internal resources to really build out their business processes properly so they were annoyed that out of the box, it didn't come "ready for them to use". My support manager explained that the entire power of the software was that it allowed every company using it to tailor the processes to suit their business. I made the call to send one of our consultants to work with them for a week onsite, at our expense to onboard them fully.

Then they tried to bring their subcontractors and client onto the system, but complained that they had to pay for it. My business development team again explained that our advertised pricing was based on a per user, per month basis and it was in fact clearly stated on the page where they signed up. Again, they weren't happy and started rejecting the invoices for the additional users.

The final straw came when the Managing Director of this small contractor demanded a meeting with myself and my boss (who happened to be the COO of $20bn global business). This gentleman had a complaint from his client that they couldn't send and receive faxes through our system. My support team tested it from our office and it worked fine. We tested it with their accounts from our office, fine again. Finally, I sent the consultant off to the client's office to test it and try to fix it.

The client didn't have a fax machine. They couldn't send or receive faxes because didn't have a fax machine.

I banged into my boss that evening at the Qantas Club lounge here in Sydney as we were both travelling. I relayed the story to him as a bit of a joke, but he looked me straight in the eye and said, "Fire them. Give them their money back in full, offer to help migrate them to a competitor, but get rid of them as a client."

I sat there perplexed, naively I'd never even thought about firing a client before.

It was a lesson that has stuck with me ever since because the truth is, we all have these horrible clients that we run across in our lives. If you're an employee in someone else's business then you just have to tolerate bad clients for the most part, but when you're in charge, no way.

Since learning that lesson there are a number of reasons why I now part ways with bad clients:

<u>People who routinely don't pay on time</u>: Last year we moved to getting paid fully in advance for all new customers because we're not a bank underwriting their cash flow. It cost us a few new customers, but it saved us tons of effort and frustration chasing late payers and writing off bad debt;

<u>Customers that are rude to my staff</u>: I have absolutely no time for people who abuse my staff. I have a special distaste for people that are nice to me, but treat my people like peasants;

<u>Clients that can't do the simplest things without help</u>: This one is a bit arbitrary, but when we pick up a client that can't complete a simple form or is logging countless tickets to achieve everything, then that's not going to be a profitable relationship; and,

<u>People who try to renegotiate our deal after we start</u>: If what we offer doesn't suit you or you need something special, I'm pretty open to finding a mutually agreeable outcome. But if you start trying to renegotiate after we start work, that doesn't fly with me.

The reality is, bad customers are expensive. They can be expensive from the perspective of doing the work for them costs more than it should and eventually it may even become unprofitable. They can also be expensive from a mental stress perspective because you spend so much time dealing with their craziness or being angry that it just ruins your mental wellbeing.

When you come across these type of customers, part ways with them. This can be really hard when you're just starting out or if the client makes up a significant portion of your revenue, so you may just have to suck it up for the short term, but plan their departure. You just need to realize that there are some clients you can never satisfy no matter how hard you try.

Depending on the situation, I often try and break up with them gently. I explain to them that I don't feel the relationship is working out and I offer to refer them to someone else who may be better suited to meeting their requirements. A number of times, I've moved them to another service provider and have had the client refer us to other potential customers. If you do this well, it can work out better for everyone.

They key to dealing with clients like this is picking them up early, analyzing why the relationship is not working well and then do what you can to remedy the situation. I also believe that I can learn something from situations like this, so take the time to try and figure it out. But once you come to a landing that it's not you, it's them, make the call quickly and pull the trigger.

Takeaway Item: Crappy clients are expensive financially, mentally and emotionally, so don't be afraid to fire them. Do your best to figure out what's wrong and fix it, but if it is obvious that it's the client, rip that band-aid off and move on.

Accountability Partners Are For Losers

I have to say that I find it totally perplexing when I see people talking about needing an "accountability partner" or someone to keep them focused and on track.

I appreciate more than most that running a business is hard work. Running an online business where you may be isolated is extra hard. It's a very lonely gig for sure.

But if you are struggling to hold yourself accountable for achieving your targets, then there is something more fundamentally broken within you.

You're looking for an emotional crutch.

I'm telling you right now to stop doing that. Figure out why you're doing what you're doing and get comfortable with it... Now!

In my experience coaching online business owners, I've run across a variety of different types of people who say they want me to help provide them with accountability.

The first group of people just confuse themselves and over complicate everything they do. They're not looking for "accountability" so much as perspective and guidance on keeping them on the right path. I often find this group are the most overwhelmed by technology and awestruck by the possibilities and potential, so they unnecessarily complicate what they are doing. I focus on keeping it simple for them.

The second group of people are a bit similar to the first, they have passion, motivation and determination, they just don't have a clue about what they should be doing. I can work with these people because again, it's not needing to be held "accountable" per se, it's more about getting help putting together their plan and realizing their possibilities.

The third group of people are the ones who are looking for someone to hold their hand and make them feel good about doing what they say they want to do. They want people to challenge them to actually get out of bed in the morning, put their pants on and get to work.

These people are looking for accountability and I can't work with these people. They're losers.

That probably sounds pretty harsh, but the reality is these people are emotionally crippled. They require a ton of external validation and convincing just to keep going forward. They are not mentally or emotionally in a place that is conducive to building a successful business of any kind. They are just draining to work with because you spend half your time playing psychologist for them.

Where to from here? Well, I'm all about solving problems and that's the point of these rules, so here we go!

If you've just read the above and aren't feeling rage and anger at how callous I am, but still see parts of your own behavior in that third group who want and need someone else to keep them accountable, then there's hope for you. You need to get a bit introspective and figure out why you need external validation. I'd be willing to bet you a warm meal that it has to do with a lack of confidence in yourself or your idea. If that's the case, harden up. You might fail, but be strong and go down swinging. And if you do fail, pick yourself up, dust yourself off and try something else because that's what winners do.

On the other hand, if you're sitting there sad and thinking that I just don't understand your #struggle or what you have to go through, then I'm afraid you've got a problem. The harsh reality is, life's not going to molly coddle you when you're feeling glum. Your competitors will smell this weakness on you and it will motivate them to work harder and eat your lunch. You don't need someone else, you need to dig down and get yourself together.

And finally, I suspect that most of you are sitting there reading this and realizing you don't need an "accountability partner", you just need some advice and perspective. Finding the right mentor, coach or mastermind group will help you immeasurably.

I'm going to close with this... Starting an online business is hard. If you're what I call a "Casual Marketer", someone with an existing job or business that is trying to branch into the online world, it's extra hard. You need to be tough to succeed. This journey will probably be as challenging as anything you've ever done. You can do it; you just have to be ready for it.

Takeaway Item: Get your emotional and mental game ready and in top shape right away because building a business online is pretty tough. You need inner strength and motivation to succeed. Other people can help by offering advice and perspective, but the accountability for achieving your goals MUST come from you!

AdSense Is Arbitrage For Stupid People

With this rule, I'm going to put it right out there... When it comes to your online business, money that you get from advertising on your site or media properties is the lowest form of monetization you can have. When you sell ads on your site, you're basically saying, "I give up on trying to monetize my own traffic."

I can already see some people reading this who are itching to tell me about how much money John Lee Dumas makes from doing ads on his podcast or how much the site "I F*cking Love Science" pulls in every month from ad networks.

I say to those people, you are wrong.

Just about every example you could foist upon me to demonstrate that this rule is incorrect is predicated on unicorn case studies. IFL Science is an exception, not the rule. If you think you could model their success with your site, "We Totally Love Geography" then I wish you the best of luck. IFL Science caught lightning in a bottle. People win the lottery all the time, but buying lottery tickets isn't a business model.

And because I'm the one writing this book and these are my rules, I secretly nestled in a counter-example that proves my own point, John Lee Dumas. His podcast gets thousands and thousands of downloads per day, so he has a very valuable audience where advertising works for him (but not necessarily his advertisers) because of scale. BUT! He makes more revenue from the other things he does (affiliate marketing and his own products) than he does from advertising.

Generating traffic and building an audience is exceptionally time consuming which means it's also expensive. If you are doing all of that effort to bring the audience in, why are you encouraging them to leave for pennies per click? It just doesn't make sense.

The other thing that is happening that you may not realize is that you're conferring status on the advertisers. When people come to your site you are establishing authority with them. As I keep saying, that's very valuable currency in the online world. When visitors see an ad or promotion on your site for something else, subconsciously they see that as an endorsement

from you. You are giving that other site or product credibility…
Again for pennies on the dollar.

And thus the rule. You deserve better.

Things like AdSense, Taboola and Outbrain profit from you
putting in all the hard work to get traffic and abdicating
responsibility for monetization. It's just a lazy form of arbitrage
that doesn't really work in your favor. It gets worse because for
the most part, those ads are horrible to look at and make your
site look terrible, so it's a double whammy for you!

You need to take down all of those ad networks from your site
straightaway. I'd venture a guess that the money they are
generating for you could be measured in less than a bag full of
Happy Meals anyway, so just let it go.

You'll note that I haven't talked about affiliate marketing at all.
I've heaped my scorn on the ad networks. That's because I
think well placed ads and promos for affiliate products are a
reasonably good way to monetize your traffic. You can vet
them, make sure the offers and products are consistent with
your brand message and when you're doing affiliate marketing

correctly, you should be able to put your hand on your heart and lend your authority with a clear conscience.

While affiliate marketing is a considerable step up from the pay per click ad networks, even that doesn't compare to having your own products and services to advertise and promote on your site.

This isn't a nice to have, this should be your core strategy.

Having your own products and services that are congruent with your content is what you should be doing because it will give you the best return on your investment. It also means that the authority and audience you are accumulating have a way of deepening their relationship with you.

There's nobody better you can recommend to your audience than you!

Takeaway Item: Doing the work of bringing people to your site only to drive them away via AdSense ads is doing yourself a disservice. Figure out a better monetization strategy than advertising arbitrage, you owe it to yourself.

It's Your House, Everyone Else Is A Guest

As I write this, it is Christmas Day and my wife is downstairs preparing dinner for us. We're having a small meal because last weekend was the big family Christmas event.

Now imagine a scenario where I invited you to my house for Christmas Dinner. You turn up late, no presents, no wine and really underdressed. We sit down for dinner, you're burping and picking at all the food. Finally, it comes time to open presents, you stand up complain about my child being spoiled and say that my wife is a bad cook.

I think it would be a safe bet that at the very minimum, I would ask you to leave our house.

That's obviously an over the top characterization, but the idea behind it is, that when someone comes to your house, they should be on their best behavior. That's just good manners and what is expected in polite society.

But those rules almost never get followed online. People wander into Facebook Groups and spam the crap out of them or just say the rudest things. Other people randomly add you to Groups or tag you in stupid ads for sunglasses. Every now and again you'll even get someone on your email list responding to you telling you that you're wrong and they know better.

Your business belongs to you. Your email list, your Facebook Groups and your Timeline are yours - they are little pieces of virtual real estate that you control. Anyone who makes use of them are visitors in your house and if they don't obey your rules and basic etiquette guidelines, then I hereby empower you to kick them out with considerable and extreme malice.

You'll undoubtedly run into the "Free Speech Police" when you start giving people the flick, but be strong. The quick fire answer is, "You have the right to remain silent". The longer answer is that "Freedom of Speech" does not give you the right to walk into my house and voice your opinion, it ensures that the government won't censor you. If they continue to act up, suggest that they take up their claim with the Supreme Court.

Lastly, dealing with trolls. I just ignore them, you should too. Clean up their mess, block them, flag them as spam, delete their posts, but don't engage with them. Responding to a troll is giving them what they want, just forget about them, cut them out like the cancer they are and move on. Nothing good comes from dealing with them!

Takeaway Item: You are the master of your domain and everyone else is there at your leisure. Do not let the inmates take over the asylum. Remove people from your online presence that are not behaving in a way that you're comfortable with.

CONCLUSION

It's kind of odd writing a conclusion for this book because when I started putting it together, I didn't really foresee there being "an end". I had originally thought of this book as a guide that I'd put together, stick it in a binder and ship it off to my Casual Marketer Monthly Newsletter subscribers. The assumption was that I'd occasionally just add a new rule, stick it in the newsletter mail out and it would keep growing.

But like most things in life, things change when you actually start digging in and doing the work. In no time at all I reached 20,000 words and decided that this guide was actually a book and I should treat it as such.

It's been a fun experience for sure. I've had these rules kicking around informally for a while but writing them down and telling the stories around them has been really helpful and beneficial for me. It's a bit like when you want to learn to write really good copy so you sit down and start writing out great ads by hand. It turns them into muscle memory.

That's what's happened with these rules. Just the process of writing this book has helped me improve my business.

I gravitate towards complex solutions as I've mentioned, it's just part of my genetic make-up I guess. The other day though I was putting together some of the ecommerce pieces of the Casual Marketer site and I'd planned out this elaborate technology solution. The problem was, it was going to take me two weeks to build it out. Worse than that, I was building things I didn't need right now.

Like an epiphany some of the rules of this book flooded my brain. I realized the mistake I was making and I tossed the whole complex solution away. I went with a simple order form and the whole thing was done in three hours... Two weeks versus three hours.

These are the kind of successes I want you to have as a result of reading this book. I want you to look at everything you do in your business and evaluate it against these rules.

Do you have crappy customers? Fire them.

Are you struggling with pricing? Just pick a price and move forward.

Do you feel like Homer Simpson? Don't Be a Homer!

And when these epiphanies happen to you and you have some successes, I want to hear about them. Send me your stories (sean@casualmarketer.com) and tell me how you're applying these rules in your life and business.

For now, that's all I've got. I hope you enjoy the book and keep me updated on your progress!

Cheers,
Sean (sean@casualmarketer.com)

Twitter: https://twitter.com/skaye
Facebook Group: https://casualmarketer.com/fb-group

BONUSES AND EXTRAS

I just wanted to remind you that I have created a bonus chapter to the book around bending social media to your will that you can download as a free gift for buying the book.

To get this bonus chapter, just head to:

https://nohyperbole.com/specialchapter

Also, I run a pretty engaging Facebook Group called, "Casual Marketer Academy" that is free to join for all of my readers, customers and students. I post in there every day across a wide variety of topics and members ask questions about their online businesses and side hustle projects.

Again, as one of my readers, I welcome you to join the group, say hello and tell us a bit about yourself!

To join the group go to:

https://casualmarketer.com/fb-group

www.ingramcontent.com/pod-product-compliance
Lightning Source LLC
Chambersburg PA
CBHW070928210326
41520CB00021B/6848